edX E-Learning Course Development

Design, develop, and deploy an interactive and informative MOOC course for the edX platform

Matthew A. Gilbert

[PACKT] open source✲
PUBLISHING   community experience distilled

BIRMINGHAM - MUMBAI

edX E-Learning Course Development

First published: May 2015

Production reference: 1270515

Published by Packt Publishing Ltd.
Livery Place
35 Livery Street
Birmingham B3 2PB, UK.

ISBN 978-1-78398-180-9

www.packtpub.com

Credits

Author
Matthew A. Gilbert

Reviewers
Rogério Theodoro de Brito

Danea Johnson

Dr. Carla Lane

Santhosh Kumar T

Commissioning Editor
Andrew Duckworth

Acquisition Editor
Subho Gupta

Content Development Editor
Sumeet Sawant

Technical Editor
Manan Patel

Copy Editors
Hiral Bhatt

Vikrant Phadke

Project Coordinator
Danuta Jones

Proofreaders
Stephen Copestake

Safis Editing

Indexer
Rekha Nair

Graphics
Abhinash Sahu

Production Coordinator
Melwyn Dsa

Cover Work
Melwyn Dsa

About the Author

Matthew A. Gilbert, MBA, is a business professor and corporate trainer with extensive experience as a writer, marketer, and speaker. He's guided by the motto "learn continuously, live generatively."

Skilled in learning management systems such as Blackboard, Canvas, eCollege, edX, and Moodle, he develops and teaches communication, management, and marketing courses for adult learners online, on campus, and in blended learning environments. In corporate settings, he conducts business communication, decision-making, and social media marketing workshops. Having embraced an opportunity overseas, Matthew now teaches undergraduates at a university in Dubai, the United Arab Emirates.

A tech-savvy writer, his first book, *edX E-Learning Course Development*, was published for educators with the aim of designing, developing, and deploying MOOC courses on the edX platform. He has also authored scholarly papers, feature articles, and Doctorious—a blog about his adventures in academia. He is an unrepentant fan of the Oxford comma; the semicolon is another one of his guilty pleasures.

As a marketer and consultant, Matthew has managed people, products, and projects in the education, entertainment, medical device, nonprofit, publishing, travel, and technology sectors. Recognized for his knowledge of social media marketing, he has been called upon to provide expert witness testimony for lawsuits and related research matters.

A charismatic speaker, Matthew uses sincerity, humor, and storytelling to connect with audiences; education, leadership, management, social media, and technology are his main topics. Be sure to ask him about his signature speech called *Superman: Manager of Steel*.

When asked why teaching is his tenure, he explains, "I embrace education as my profession because it empowers me to help shape the lives of others, while giving my own life greater meaning."

For more information about Matthew, you can visit his website at matthewagilbert.com, connect with him on LinkedIn at linkedin.com/in/matthewagilbert, or follow him on Twitter at @MatthewAGilbert.

This book was written over many months and a multitude of miles: from California to Dubai, Abu Dhabi, Oman, and even 38,000 feet above the Arctic Circle on an Emirates Airbus A380! However, without the insight, input, and inspiration from the following individuals, this book wouldn't have happened.
To each of you and to those whom I might have inadvertently not included, I extend my heartfelt gratitude. Thank you!

Anant Agarwal

Anastassia Konovalova

Andy Armstrong

Ashish Bhanushali

Binny K. Babu

Carla Lane

Danea Johnson

Dani Babb

Dani Perkins

Daniel Hayek

Dominique Samario

Garrett Gatch

Gregory Calo

Helen Vitaris

Jacob Gilbert

John K. Rounds

Kiran Patil

Laurie Andutan

Manan Patel

Marietta Poshi

Mario A. González

Max Gilbert

Meggie Windari

Michael Ball

Ned Batchelder

Nikhil Chinnari

Petar Apostolov

Philip Guo

Piotr Mitros

Rae Lynn Estrada

Rogério Brito

Rosalind Englander-Calo

Santhosh Kumar T.

Satinder K. Dhiman

Saunya Berger McDaniel

Shamikh Siddiqui

Shandee Rae

Sharon Dunigan Jumper

Steve DiCasa

Subho Gupta

Sumeet Sawant

Szilvia Beylik

Tania Nathan

Tihomir Davchev

About the Reviewers

Rogério Theodoro de Brito has a BSc in computer science and an MSc in computational biology, both from the University of São Paulo, Brazil. Academically, he likes graph theory, combinatorial optimization, and discrete mathematics. He teaches various subjects in computer science and IT at Mackenzie Presbyterian University, São Paulo, and is an enthusiast of both education (MOOCs in particular) and free software.

Rogério has been contributing to the Debian project (`debian.org`) since 2005 and has been an official Debian maintainer since 2008, maintaining about 20 software packages (also available for the popular Ubuntu Linux and Linux Mint). At the intersection of MOOCs, education, and free software, he is the coauthor of coursera-dl (`https://github.com/coursera-dl/coursera`) and edx-dl (`https://github.com/shk3/edx-downloader`), which are designed to facilitate learners to access the course material from Coursera and edX respectively.

You can see his blog at `http://cynic.cc/blog/`.

Danea Johnson is a communications and sales specialist in the technology field with 5 years of higher education, leadership, and experience in curriculum development. She developed her love for teaching during her first part-time job as a gymnastics instructor at the age of 14. Later, she spent years assisting in instructional technology for diverse groups at several educational institutions, ranging from arts students from universities to impoverished high-school students with learning difficulties. Danea enjoys being creative, getting to know people and how they learn, and finding new ways to communicate and teach things that impact lives.

I would like to sincerely thank Mr. Gilbert for being incredibly warm and welcoming, providing me with his advice as I sought after my own career goals, and for granting me the opportunity to take part in this wonderful project.

Dr. Carla Lane has an extensive background in distance learning and the evaluation of mediated educational programs. She is the executive director of The Education Coalition, a nonprofit group that provides educational evaluation services for districts, universities, and other entities requiring local, state, and national evaluations. She has been extensively involved in the field of education through her research in distance learning. Her work has been published in many research reports and journals. Carla has authored three textbooks on educational technology and distance learning. Now, she conducts research in online instructional strategies for men and women in active military and veterans and their spouses for the Federal Government Distance Learning Association (FGDLA), where she is the vicepresident of the higher education sector.

Carla was recently named a Research Fellow by the University of Phoenix, and conducts research in online mentoring at the doctoral level. This research is part of a grant from the university. She has taught online for the university since 1991 and has received the Quality Award for her work.

For 15 years, Carla was with WestEd — a regional educational laboratory — as a senior researcher. She was also the project director of the Star Schools dissemination project — the Distance Learning Resource Network (DLRN).

She is a master trainer in distance learning for UCLA and teaches in several doctoral programs that involve specialization in educational technology and instructional design for online learning. She has written for, and has been funded for grants through, Star Schools, PBS Mathline and PBS TeacherLine, Challenge, NTIA, TIIAP, the California Department of Education, the California Community College Chancellor's Office, the United States Department of Justice, the Los Angeles County Office of Education, and NASA.

Carla earned a doctorate in education (educational leadership research design/ statistics, adult education, and educational technology) from the University of Missouri-St. Louis, an MA in mass communication from Webster University, and a Bachelor of Science in English from Washington University, St. Louis, Missouri. She also holds a degree in broadcast engineering.

Santhosh Kumar T. has spent more than a decade exploring the nuances of the online learning environment. Currently a learning consultant at Dexler Information Solutions, he uses his rich experience to help train managers so that they can understand which solution works best for them.

A commerce graduate from Bangalore University, Santhosh followed his passion for multimedia, beginning as a novice learner and progressing to an expert, with a wide range of technical qualifications that span the spectrum of content development. His strength lies in being a self-starter who needs no external motivation to learn new technologies. He uses his knowledge of various content authoring tools and couples it with interactive multimedia design to create engaging content for his organization.

Santhosh has worked with companies such as Purpleframe Technologies, Epiance, and Mentorware India. He is an avid reader who loves to spend his free time reading and listening to music—both oldies and the latest tracks. Nonetheless, it is just as much a holiday for him to spend his time learning what the world is doing in the field of online education and coming back with ideas in this field.

Dexler Information Solutions is a learning solutions provider that leverages technology to enable companies and institutions to manage and enhance their knowledge pool. Dexler's endeavor has been to provide strategic educational services and products, developed on robust delivery platforms using innovative learning enablers. Dexler is recognized for offering customized learning content in a flexible framework for individual learning, corporate education, and community training. It has evolved from an instructor-led training (ILT) organization to a complete integrated learning solutions provider. Dexler believes in being gamechangers for their customers and providing customized solutions that enhance their businesses.

www.PacktPub.com

Support files, eBooks, discount offers, and more

For support files and downloads related to your book, please visit www.PacktPub.com.

Did you know that Packt offers eBook versions of every book published, with PDF and ePub files available? You can upgrade to the eBook version at www.PacktPub.com and as a print book customer, you are entitled to a discount on the eBook copy. Get in touch with us at service@packtpub.com for more details.

At www.PacktPub.com, you can also read a collection of free technical articles, sign up for a range of free newsletters and receive exclusive discounts and offers on Packt books and eBooks.

https://www2.packtpub.com/books/subscription/packtlib

Do you need instant solutions to your IT questions? PacktLib is Packt's online digital book library. Here, you can search, access, and read Packt's entire library of books.

Why subscribe?

- Fully searchable across every book published by Packt
- Copy and paste, print, and bookmark content
- On demand and accessible via a web browser

Free access for Packt account holders

If you have an account with Packt at www.PacktPub.com, you can use this to access PacktLib today and view 9 entirely free books. Simply use your login credentials for immediate access.

This book is dedicated to my sons, Jacob and Max. You are my greatest teachers, my favorite students, and my most edXceptional inspirations!

Table of Contents

Preface

edX is an open source learning management system (LMS) and course authoring tool launched by Harvard University and the Massachusetts Institute of Technology (MIT) as a nonprofit partnership. A massively online open course (MOOC) platform, edX offers students self-paced learning, online discussion groups, Wiki-based collaborative learning, assessment of learning, online laboratories, and other interactive learning tools.

If you're an educator creating a course for edX, or a corporate trainer using Open edX to achieve learning and development initiatives, then *edX E-Learning Course Development* is ideal for you. Whether you're developing an online course for the first time or you are a veteran LMS scholar, this book gets you up and running with edX.

Walking you through eight essential steps for creating an edX course, each chapter signifies a step in the curriculum development and implementation process. We begin with an overview of MOOCs and the history of edX, detail curriculum development and video production best practices, and then explore exercises and assessment options. We then integrate everything, managing your edX course's administrative options while facilitating your students' learning experience. Finally, we suggest strategies to market your course using traditional tools, edX's internal options, and social media.

What this book covers

Chapter 1, Getting Started, introduces edX and reviews your role and responsibilities helping you to discover best practices in the process. You will be guided through the process of signing up for edX, creating a Studio account, and taking the first steps towards creating your first course.

Chapter 2, Planning the Curriculum, concerns planning your course's curriculum and understanding the elements within edX necessary for launching it.

You will learn about the edX Course Matrix, and how to prepare your course's About page, write the various preliminary documents for your course, improve your knowledge of learning sequences, design exercises and assessments, choose textbooks and materials, moderate the discussion forum, launch your course's Wiki, and finally, preview the necessary information for the certificate of mastery.

Chapter 3, Producing Videos, explores the idea and intent of instructional videos to your course, presents video production pointers, reviews post-production processes, explains the process of transcript creation, and outlines how to create playlists on YouTube for each of your courses.

Chapter 4, Designing Exercises, demonstrates how to develop exercises, discusses ways to engage students, reviews problem components, and explains interactive exercises. You will also learn about four problem types: general exercises and tools, image-based exercises and tools, multiple-choice exercises and tools, and STEM exercises and tools. A/B split tests, in conjunction with content experiments, are also explored.

Chapter 5, Integrating the Curriculum, focuses on course components where your curriculum converges, introduces integration of curriculum, and presents practices that enrich your students' learning experiences. You will also establish your course outline, define course sections, include course subsections, input course units, develop course components, add pages, upload files, post updates and handouts, upload PDF textbooks, and address accessibility issues.

Chapter 6, Administering Your Course, outlines administrative functions, best practices, and online resources that make your job easier. You will also learn how to establish a grading policy, control content visibility, include student cohorts, tackle beta testing, export and import your course, make the most of edX resources, and finally, launch your course.

Chapter 7, Facilitating Your Course, offers insight into assigning staff roles, inviting students to enroll, directing your discussions, managing your messaging, creating your course wiki, reviewing course data, supervising student data, overseeing answer data, managing the gradebook, and issuing course completion certificates.

Chapter 8, Promoting Your Course, shares strategies for marketing your edX course before it is offered, and shows you how to create networking opportunities for your students after it concludes. In this chapter, you get to tackle traditional marketing tools, identify options from edX, discuss social media marketing, explore the basics of personal branding, review marketing metrics, and define the role of student feedback.

What you need for this book

XBlock is the SDK for the edX MOOC platform, which is written primarily in Python 2. It is a component architecture that enables developers to create independent course components — XBlocks — that will work seamlessly with other components in an online course. Course authors can combine XBlocks from various sources, including text, video, Wikis, and online laboratories.

You can access the edX open source platform technology along with platform developments from Stanford, Harvard, MIT, edX, and other contributors at openedx.org. If you plan to run Open edX, you will be pleased to know that there are hosting providers, or you can install and run the software on your own server. However, edX does not provide direct support for independent installations. If you are a developer who wants to get involved with edX, you can find its technical details at openedx.org, including documentation, source code repositories, mailing lists, and IRC channels.

Who this book is for

If you are an educator who is creating a course for edX, or a corporate trainer using Open edX for learning and development initiatives, then *edX E-Learning Course Development* is the ideal book for you. Whether you are developing an online course for the first time or you are a veteran LMS scholar, this book will get you up and running with edX.

Conventions

In this book, you will find a number of text styles that distinguish between different kinds of information. Here are some examples of these styles and an explanation of their meaning.

Code words in text, database table names, folder names, filenames, file extensions, pathnames, dummy URLs, user input, and Twitter handles are shown as follows: "It is formatted as HH:MM:SS, and its maximum value is 23:59:59."

New terms and **important words** are shown in bold. Words that you see on the screen, for example, in menus or dialog boxes, appear in the text like this: "Clicking on **Check** reveals whether the answer is correct or not."

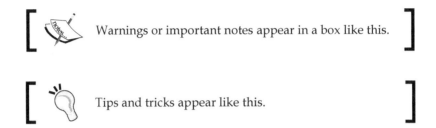

Reader feedback

Feedback from our readers is always welcome. Let us know what you think about this book—what you liked or disliked. Reader feedback is important for us as it helps us develop titles that you will really get the most out of.

To send us general feedback, simply e-mail `feedback@packtpub.com`, and mention the book's title in the subject of your message.

If there is a topic that you have expertise in and you are interested in either writing or contributing to a book, see our author guide at `www.packtpub.com/authors`.

Customer support

Now that you are the proud owner of a Packt book, we have a number of things to help you to get the most from your purchase.

Downloading the color images of this book

We also provide you with a PDF file that has color images of the screenshots and diagrams used in this book. The color images will help you better understand the changes in the output. You can download this file from `https://www.packtpub.com/sites/default/files/downloads/1809OS_ColoredImages.pdf`.

Errata

Although we have taken every care to ensure the accuracy of our content, mistakes do happen. If you find a mistake in one of our books—maybe a mistake in the text or the code—we would be grateful if you could report this to us. By doing so, you can save other readers from frustration and help us improve subsequent versions of this book. If you find any errata, please report them by visiting http://www.packtpub.com/submit-errata, selecting your book, clicking on the **Errata Submission Form** link, and entering the details of your errata. Once your errata are verified, your submission will be accepted and the errata will be uploaded to our website or added to any list of existing errata under the Errata section of that title.

To view the previously submitted errata, go to https://www.packtpub.com/books/content/support and enter the name of the book in the search field. The required information will appear under the **Errata** section.

Piracy

Piracy of copyrighted material on the Internet is an ongoing problem across all media. At Packt, we take the protection of our copyright and licenses very seriously. If you come across any illegal copies of our works in any form on the Internet, please provide us with the location address or website name immediately so that we can pursue a remedy.

Please contact us at copyright@packtpub.com with a link to the suspected pirated material.

We appreciate your help in protecting our authors and our ability to bring you valuable content.

eBooks, discount offers, and more

Did you know that Packt offers eBook versions of every book published, with PDF and ePub files available? You can upgrade to the eBook version at www.PacktPub.com and as a print book customer, you are entitled to a discount on the eBook copy. Get in touch with us at customercare@packtpub.com for more details.

At www.PacktPub.com, you can also read a collection of free technical articles, sign up for a range of free newsletters, and receive exclusive discounts and offers on Packt books and eBooks.

Questions

If you have a problem with any aspect of this book, you can contact us at
questions@packtpub.com, and we will do our best to address the problem.

1
Getting Started

Curiosity is the engine of achievement.

According to Sir Ken Robinson—a leader in creativity, innovation, and human resource development—curiosity drives our desire to acquire knowledge. This educational exploration leads us to a deeper understanding of human creativity and intelligence.

Whether you are teaching in a traditional classroom or online in a learning management system, as an educator, it's your task to cultivate your students' curiosity. As education has evolved into an increasingly interactive experience, new online options have emerged to facilitate this function.

One emerging option is a **Massive Open Online Course** (**MOOC**). As defined by the Oxford Dictionary, a MOOC is "a course of study made available over the Internet without charge to a very large number of people." A nonprofit partnership between Harvard University and Massachusetts Institute of Technology (MIT), edX is a MOOC platform designed to engage your students' curiosity while activating the engine of their achievement.

Here is a screenshot of the edX home page, which you can find at `http://edx.org`:

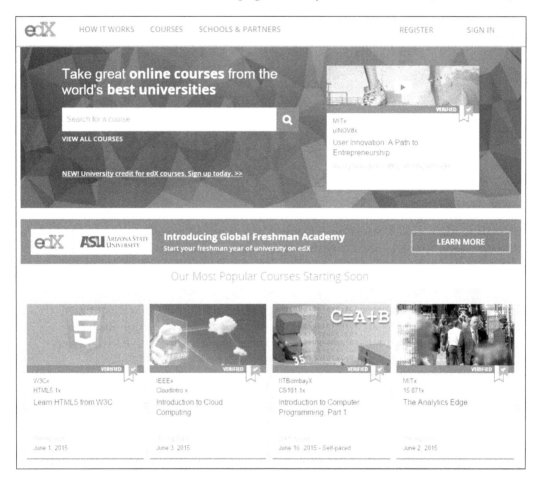

This book walks you through the steps to create your first course with edX. By the time you finish this book, you should be able to develop or adapt the curriculum, produce instructional videos, design exercises and assessments, administer your course, and facilitate your students' learning experience while marketing it on social media.

Organized sequentially, each chapter represents a progressive step in the curriculum development and implementation process. To get started, we will cover the following topics in this first chapter:

- Review edX's potential and purpose
- Define your role and responsibilities

- Explore available edX courses
- Create your edX user account
- Explain signing up for Studio
- Outline the creation of your course
- Preview your course's characteristics

edX's potential and purpose

Understanding the potential of edX requires a realization of online learning trends. Let's consider the 2014 Babson Survey Research Group survey of online learning, *Grade Level: Tracking Online Education in the United States*. The survey found the following facts:

- 3.7 percent more students enrolled in at least one distance-education course in 2014 than in the previous year. This is the slowest rate of increase in over 10 years, but the pace of online learning accounts for almost three quarters of all increases in enrollment to higher education in the United States.

- 70.8 percent of chief academic officers agree that online education is critical to their institution's long-term strategy, a 48.8 percent growth from 2002.

- 80.9 percent of for-profit institutions report that online education is critical to their long-term strategy. 72.9 percent of public institutions and 63.5 percent of private nonprofit institutions report the same.

Survey data for MOOCs shows that they have promise, but present unique challenges. This makes sense, given their relative newness in the online-learning landscape, along with their increased scale and scope. Findings from the survey indicate the following facts:

- 8.0 percent of higher-education institutions currently have a MOOC, up from 2.6 percent in 2012 and 5.0 percent in 2013

- 16.3 percent of academic leaders believe MOOCs offer a sustainable method of offering courses online, a drop from 28.3 percent in 2012

- 39.9 percent of academic institutions are still undecided about MOOCs, while 46.5 percent have no immediate plans to launch a MOOC

 You can download the 2014 Babson Survey Research Group (BSRG) survey of online learning, *Grade Level: Tracking Online Education in the United States*, from `http://onlinelearningconsortium.org/read/survey-reports-2014/`.

Growth of the MOOC market

Despite the mixed results from the Babson Survey Research Group report, there is much about MOOCs that is positive. Both educational institutions and private organizations are exploring ways to meet their learning objectives with MOOCs.

A January 2015 report by Visiongain, an independent business information provider for the telecoms, pharmaceutical, defense, energy, and metal industries, anticipates the worldwide revenue from MOOCs will reach $1.5 billion in 2015.

The findings of the report, *Massive Open Online Course (MOOC) Market 2015-2020: mEducation, Distance, Open & e-Learning in Higher Education & Enterprise*, were based on the growing use of mobile devices, increasing rates of enrollment in MOOC courses, the growing use of MOOCs for enterprise-level training, and a strong demand for low-cost, high-quality globalized education.

 You can review the summary and table of contents of the Visiongain MOOC report at `http://www.reportlinker.com/p02720992-summary/Massive-Open-Online-Course-MOOC-Market-mEducation-Distance-Open-e-Learning-in-Higher-Education-Enterprise.html`.

Likewise, in a December 2014 EdSurge article, *MOOCs in 2014: Breaking Down the Numbers*, Dhawal Shah shares similarly compelling statistics supporting MOOCs:

- The top three subjects in which students enrolled include humanities, computer science and programming, and business and management.

- The top five MOOC providers by student enrollment are Coursera (10.5 million), edX (3 million), Udacity (1.5 million), MiradaX (1 million), and FutureLearn (800,000). You can review a list of courses offered by each MOOC provider at `https://www.class-central.com/providers`.

- The number of top 25 United States universities included in the US News World Report rankings offering courses online for free has grown to 22.

- The number of universities now offering MOOCs has doubled to 400.

- The number of cumulative MOOC courses doubled to 2,400.

Shah's article indicates that, while MOOCs are in a phase of early adoption, they are on the precipice of pronounced growth. There are already intriguing examples of what the future holds for MOOCs. Top trends include the following:

- MOOC providers offering credentials for their paid courses

- Increased focus on the quality of course videos and materials

- A shift to an on-demand model of delivery, such as lynda.com and Udemy, in which a student can complete a course at their pace, and not in alignment with a traditional academic quarter or semester

The emergence of Open edX

Another intriguing evolution acknowledged in Shah's article is that Open edX—the open source version of edX—has emerged as the preferred MOOC platform for organizations and groups. It has already been adopted by organizations in locations such as Jordan, Japan, France, China, India, and the United States.

> You can read Dhawal Shah's article, *MOOCs in 2014: Breaking Down the Numbers*, online at https://www.edsurge.com/n/2014-12-26-moocs-in-2014-breaking-down-the-numbers.

Further strengthening the standing of Open edX among organizations, November 2014 saw the launch of a conference for developing and using the edX open source platform. Hosted by the Open edX community in Cambridge, Massachusetts, the conference welcomed developers, system administrators, education specialists, and anyone working with or wanting to learn more about Open EdX.

> You can learn more about the Open edX Conference at http://con.openedx.org, review slides, or watch YouTube videos of the presentations online at https://openedx.atlassian.net/wiki/display/OPEN/Open+edX+Conference+Presentations.

Emerging educational opportunities

MOOCs are also making inroads into higher education. In 2013, Georgia Institute of Technology announced plans to offer an online MS degree in computer science. Powered by Udacity's MOOC platform and offered in partnership with AT&T, the program—informally called "OMS CS"—is estimated to cost $7,000, a fraction of an equivalent on-campus program. Enrollment opened in January 2015, with the first cohort of classes beginning that fall.

> You can learn more about the Georgia Institute of Technology "OMS CS" program at http://www.omscs.gatech.edu.

MOOCs are making their mark in emerging educational markets. In March 2015, the US Agency for International Development (USAID) and `CourseTalk.com`, an online course review company, launched of a two-year, 1.55-million-dollar initiative, Advancing MOOCs for Development, to expand education and career training globally.

As part of the initiative, the Technology and Social Change Group (TASCHA) at the University of Washington will analyze more than 70,000 CourseTalk student reviews to understand the awareness and usage of MOOCs among 18- to 35-year olds in Colombia, the Philippines, and South Africa. IREX, a nonprofit development organization, will provide support for the program.

The research will be used to design a MOOC-centric training framework and create a campaign to increase MOOC enrollment and completion rates in those countries.

 You can learn more about the Advancing MOOCs for Development program at `http://www.coursetalk.com/advancingmooc`.

Another unique way MOOCs can be used is a **Small Private Online Course** (**SPOC**). SPOCs are basically smaller-scale versions of MOOCs that are used with on-campus students or special interest groups who want to share knowledge. SPOCs work well with a flipped classroom approach, combining online interaction with resources in conjunction with real-time engagement in a classroom.

The impact of edX

Founded in May 2012 as a partnership between Harvard University and Massachusetts Institute of Technology (MIT), edX has established itself as one of the leading MOOC platforms. edX is currently led by CEO Anant Agarwal, PhD, who taught the first edX course on circuits and electronics from MIT; 155,000 students from 162 countries were enrolled.

 You can watch a YouTube video of Anant Agarwal explaining how edX works: `https://youtu.be/B-EFayAA5_0`.

Working from MIT's OpenCourseWare initiative, edX is unique among MOOCs as the only one that is both nonprofit and open source (a feature it released in June 2013). Dedicated to a desire to democratize education, edX was designed for students and institutions seeking to transform themselves using leading technology, innovative pedagogy, and rigorous courses, regardless of location, gender, income, or social status.

Learn more about Open edX in this video from ExtensionEngine, a team of passionate engineers, designers and product managers focused on making a difference in online and blended education: `https://youtu.be/yDE8vN6DI_k`. You can also learn about the services they offer to assist you in the implementation of your edX course at `http://extensionengine.com/services/open-edx/`.

As of January 2015, edX has more than 10 million course enrollments, with more than 3 million students from every country. Approximately 70 percent of edX students come from outside the U.S. edX learners range in age from 8 to 95, with a student body consisting of 60 percent continuing learners, 24 percent university-age learners, and 4 percent high-school students which comprise edX's High School Initiative.

A powerful platform, edX can enhance education both on-campus and online. To achieve that goal, in September 2013, edX partnered with Google to build `MOOC.org`—a free, open-source platform for universities, institutions, businesses, and individuals to create courses on the cloud. Still in development, this project will very likely revolutionize online learning just as WordPress reimagined online publishing.

The previously mentioned 4 percent enrollment of high school students reflects edX's High School Initiative, which it launched in September 2014. Students can enroll in AP-level courses on subjects including English, history, mathematics, and science, among others. Teachers can also use the materials of these courses to supplement their classroom curriculum. Students can take a course for free or pay for a Verified Certificate to share with teachers or college admissions.

 Learn more about edX's High School Initiative at `https://www.edx.org/high-school-initiative`

October 2014 saw the addition of professional development courses to edX. Designed for working professionals, these courses offer students a convenient, time-saving online learning experience that fits into their busy schedules. Courses can run for a few days to several weeks. Content is geared to a specific industry or skill set, with an emphasis on hands-on scenarios from the field. All professional education courses are fee-based; the fees vary by course. Many offer continuing education or professional education credit, and all courses give students the option for Verified Certificates of Achievement.

 Learn more about edX's professional development courses at `https://www.edx.org/professional-education`

Around the same time edX launched the professional development courses, they announced that they were beginning to offer their partners the ability to host their courses on a white-labeled site, branded by the institution and powered by the edX platform. You can look for this option to emerge more actively over time.

Explore an example of edX's white label initiative via MIT Professional Education's course *Tackling the Challenges of Big Data* at `https://mitprofessionalx.mit.edu` and *Energy Technology and Policy* from UT Austin at `https://utaustinx.edx.org`.

In March 2015, edX partnered with Microsoft to make courses available for individuals wanting to build innovative applications, services, and experiences on the Microsoft platform. Initial courses include Programming with C#, Introduction to TypeScript, Introduction to Bootstrap, Querying with Transact SQL, Building Cloud Apps with Microsoft Azure, Introduction to Office 365 APIs, and Windows PowerShell Fundamentals.

Explore edX at `https://www.edx.org` or get started with Open edX at `https://open.edx.org`. Learn about edX's High School Initiative at `https://www.edx.org/high-school-initiative`, its partnership with Microsoft at `https://www.edx.org/school/microsoft`, and professional education programs at `https://www.edx.org/professional-education`.

In April 2015 edX announced the Global Freshman Academy (GFA), a partnership with Arizona State University (ASU). This one of a kind collaboration lets learners worldwide earn freshman-level university credit after passing a series of digital immersion courses. Courses are designed and taught by ASU faculty, while being hosted by edX. There are no application, transcript, no GPA requirements, and no entrance exams. Plus, you only pay for credit when you pass! The result is a reimagined freshman year that's accessible, cost-effective, and personalized.

Learn more about the Global Freshman Academy and sign up for email notifications about GFA updates and new courses at `https://www.edx.org/gfa`. You can also watch the video *Getting Started Global Freshman Academy* at `https://youtu.be/4DDBoI92NoE`

April 2015 also saw the introduction of a long awaited edX mobile app for both Android and iPhone. Notably, the edX mobile app does not offer full functionality; it is basically a companion to the `edx.org` website. You can use it to download course videos and watch them later, even without an Internet connection. However, you will need to use a web browser on a computer to access the rest of the course, including course discussions, homework, and quizzes.

 Learn more about the edX mobile app at `https://www.edx.org/blog/learn-go-edx-mobile-app` or view instructions on using the app on the online edX Guide for Students at `http://edx-guide-for-students.readthedocs.org/en/latest/SFD_mobile.html`

The foundation and future of edX

39 charter member colleges and universities support edX's mission, including the founding members, MIT and Harvard, and other leading academic institutions comprising the xConsortium. Another 32 universities, NGOs, businesses, and high-profile quality course builders represent the member institutions.

 You can view the list of edX members at `https://www.edx.org/schools-partners`.

As of May 2015, edX has produced 518 courses: 125 are currently available, 67 more will start soon, 82 are upcoming, and 55 are self-paced; 244 have been archived. Courses cover topics that include biology, business, chemistry, computer science, economics, finance, electronics, engineering, history, humanities, law, literature, math, medicine, music, nutrition, philosophy, physics, science, statistics, and more. edX, HarvardX, and MITx have successfully piloted several SPOCs as well.

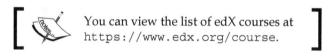 You can view the list of edX courses at `https://www.edx.org/course`.

EdX was designed to not only deliver education but also revolutionize learning. Given that goal, edX seeks to understand how students learn, how technology can transform learning, and the ways in which teachers teach. Team members are tasked to analyze data from each course, evaluating mouse clicks, time spent on tasks, how students engage assessments, and other metrics. The short-term goal is to improve a course, but the larger goal is to understand how to best leverage technology for learning.

edX embraces four principles: operate as a nonprofit organization, remain an open source platform, embrace collaboration, and achieve financial stability. The questions edX seeks to answer include the following:

- What motivates students to learn and persist?
- What helps students retain knowledge?
- What are the best ways to teach complex ideas?
- How can we assess what students have learned?
- What is best taught in person versus online?

You might find it helpful to keep the preceding questions in mind when developing and teaching your edX courses.

Your role and responsibilities

Like Paul Revere and his midnight ride, we're in the midst of a revolution—an educational revolution—with its beginnings in Boston. As an online educator, you're leading the charge for change, with edX as your weapon of mass instruction! As you begin your march forward, consider keeping the cadence outlined in the following best practices:

- Allocate sufficient time and resources; it will take time to conceptualize and create the curriculum and instructional videos for your course.
- Assemble a team of instructional designers, graphic designers, software developers, student volunteers, teaching assistants, videographers, and other skilled professionals to help you develop curricula, review exercises, and manage your course.
- Convert a typical 8- to 16-week on-campus course into several smaller units.
- Develop your curriculum in modules. Doing this integrates your course with the structure of edX sections and subsections, while aligning your instruction in a way students prefer to learn. This also makes it easier to revise, rearrange, or remove content when you update the course.
- Leverage edX's functionality to enhance the interactivity of your curriculum, while making it as rigorous as an on-campus course. Just because your course is online doesn't mean it should be less academically intense.
- Limit your videos to 3 to 5 minutes in length. According to `StatisticBrain.com`, the average length of time people will watch an Internet video is just 2.7 minutes. Therefore, shorter is better.

- Participate in the user community. There are three online resources: edX Author Support, the edx-code Google group, and the XBlock Google group.

- Replace your classroom lecture with a learning sequence. Interweave what edX calls finger exercises within a video lecture sequence. This translates into short assessments usually with one to five questions.

- Select subject matter experts for your team whose expertise you can integrate into your curricula. Have them review your material for accuracy and rigor.

- Teach in the same student-centered way as you've always done. Although edX is unique, the andragogical principles you've used when teaching adults and the pedagogical approaches you've used when teaching kids still apply.

 You can access edX Course Author Support at `http://help.edge.edx.org`, join the edx-code Google group at `https://groups.google.com/forum/#!forum/edx-code`, or participate in the XBlock Google group at `https://groups.google.com/forum/#!forum/edx-xblock`.

Creating your edX account

While you don't need an edX account to see the list of courses, you do need it to take a course. Beyond the immediate benefit of taking a course on `edX.org`, as an instructor you will learn best practices from other educators who are already using the platform. If haven't created an account already while exploring the courses in the preceding sections, follow these steps to get started:

1. Go to `www.edx.org`.

2. Click on the blue **Register** link in the top-right corner of the page.

3. Complete the registration form, mentioning the following:
    ° **Email**
    ° **Full Name**
    ° **Public Username**

 Note that your public username will appear in any discussions or forums you participate in, and it cannot be changed later.

   ° **Password**
   ° **Country**

- ° **Gender**
- ° **Year of Birth**
- ° **Highest Level of Education Completed**
- ° **Mailing Address**
- ° **Tell us why you're interested in edX**

4. Agree to the Terms of Service and Honor Code.
5. Click on the blue **Create your account** button.

6. Change your account settings by clicking **Account Settings** under the downward arrow to the right of your username in the top-right corner of the page, like this:

7. Change your **Basic Account Information** including **Full Name**, **Email Address**, **Password**, **Language**, and **Country or Region**.

 You cannot change your Username after you create your account.

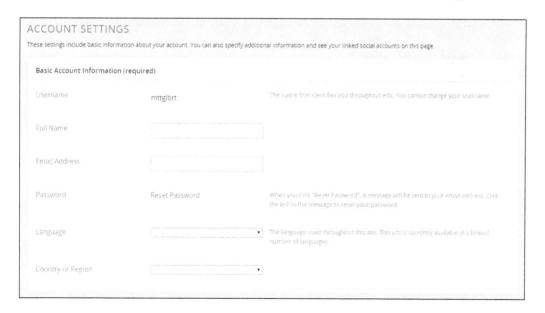

8. Change your **Connected Accounts** by linking or unlinking your **Facebook** and **Google** accounts with your edX account, as follows:

9. Change your profile by clicking **My Profile** under the downward arrow to the right of your username in the top-right corner of the page.

10. Click on the **Upload an image** icon to add a profile picture, and click inside the **+ About me** box to enter information about yourself for other edX users to read.

You must specify your birth year in your **Account Settings** before you can share your full profile. Until you do so, you can only share a **Limited Profile**.

11. Review your profile picture and **About me** bio, clicking on either to change them.

12. Sign out of your account by clicking **Sign Out** on the downward arrow to the right of your username in the top-right corner of the page.

Your students will follow steps similar to those explained previously to register for edX and enroll in your course. After registering, all that a student needs to take an edX course is a computer or a mobile device, and a willingness to learn.

Students can audit your course for personal enrichment, or they can pay to receive a certificate of achievement by earning a passing grade. There is no penalty for failing to complete assignments or discontinuing their participation in a course they choose to audit.

In addition, fundamental to the edX student experience is the Honor Code. Similar to those at traditional academic institutions, the edX Honor Code defines the ethical expectations from students. When enrolling in a course, students pledge to do the following:

- Complete all mid-term and final exams with only their own work. They must not submit the work of any other person.
- Maintain only one user account and not let anyone else use their username or password.
- Not engage in any activity that would dishonestly improve their results, or improve or hurt the results of others.
- Not post answers to problems that are being used to assess student performance.

Creating a collaborative community of learning is also essential to edX. Unless instructors give different direction, students in an edX course are encouraged to carry out these actions:

- Collaborate with others on lecture videos, exercises, homework, and labs
- Discuss general concepts and material of each course with others
- Present ideas and written work to fellow edX learners or others for comments or criticism

Exploring edX courses

Now that you've understood the potential and purpose of edX along with your role and responsibilities, let's familiarize ourselves with where to find edX courses.

Finding courses by navigating

1. Go to `www.edx.org`.
2. Click on **Find Courses** shown at the top of the page.

3. Review the course list that shows up as shown in the following screenshot:

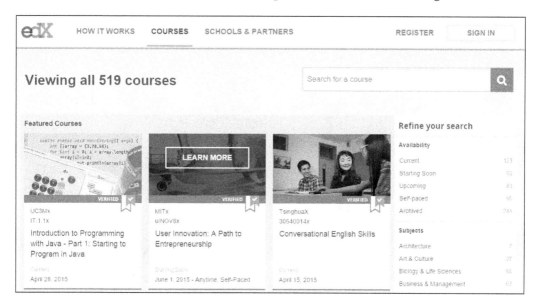

4. Hover over each course until the **Learn More** graphic appears. Click on it to view the course's About page; it should look something like this:

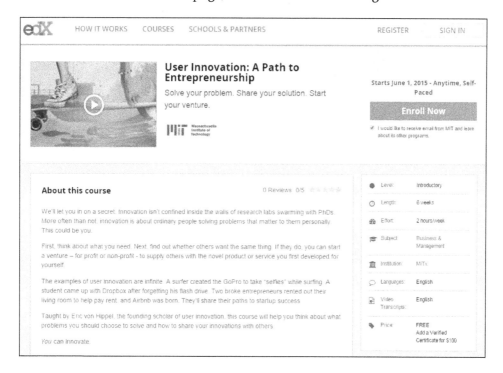

5. Review the information about the course and watch the course's intro video in the top-left corner of the course's About page, as shown in the following screenshot.

6. Click on the green **Enroll Now** button on the upper right-hand corner of the About page to enroll in the course.

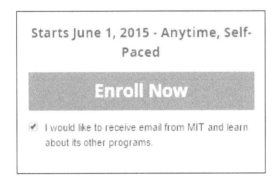

7. Share the course information on social media using the sharing buttons provided.

8. Create an account (if you don't have one already) using your Facebook or Google+ account or fill in the form, making sure to agree to the edX **Terms of Service and Honor Code**.

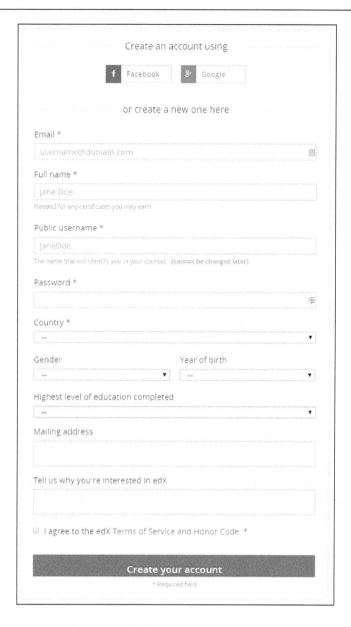

9. Hover over the white **Sign in** button until it turns blue and click it if you already have an edX account.

10. Sign in by entering your **Email** and **Password** or with your Facebook or Google+ account.

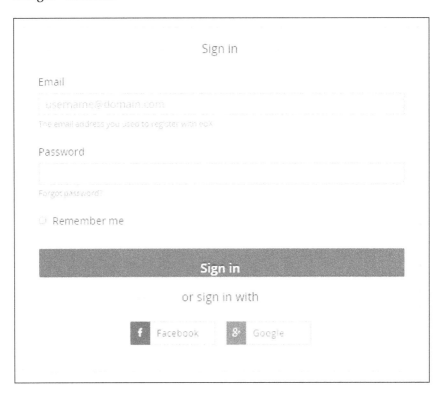

11. Click on the green **Pursue a Verified Certificate** button if you want to earn a certificate if that option is available. Click on the blue **Audit This Course** button if you prefer to take the course for enrichment, but without earning a certificate.

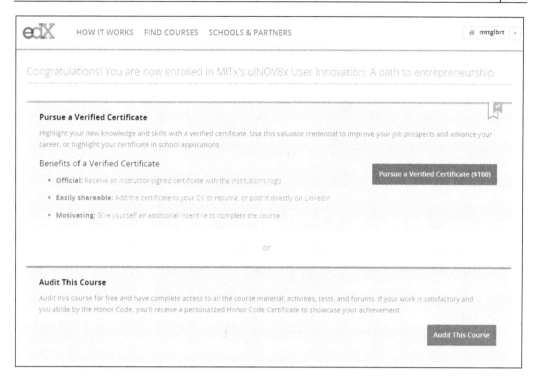

12. View your most recent course enrollment at the top of your list of **Current Courses** that displays.

13. Decide whether you want to make a donation to edX in the field in the top-right corner of the page if that is offered; a $5 donation is suggested.

14. Consider converting your enrollment from **Audit** to **Verified** by signing up for an **ID verified Certificate of Achievement** for this course.

15. Scroll down the page to see the **Dashboard** of your **Current Courses**.

16. Access your currently available courses by clicking on the blue **View Course** button, as shown here:

17. Access your completed courses by clicking the gray **View Archived Course** button.

18. Click the gear icon to the left of the blue **View Course** button or the gray **View Archived Course** to **Unenroll** from a course.

19. Click the gear icon to the left of the blue **View Course** button or the gray **View Archived Course** to change your **Email Settings** for a course.

20. Click the white **Dashboard** button in the top-right corner of any page outside of an edX course to see the Dashboard of your **Current Courses**.

Finding courses by searching

1. Go to `www.edx.org`.

2. Enter a search word or phrase; a list of suggested matches will open beneath the search box.

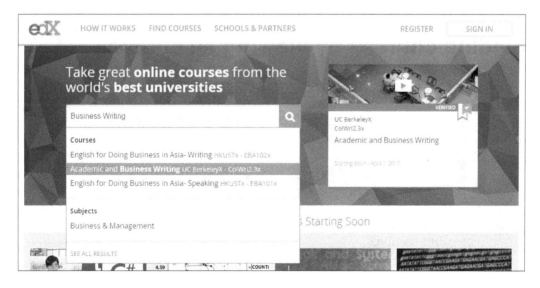

3. Select a suggested result if correct, or click the search icon for additional results.

4. Review the course list that displays.

5. Hover over each course until the **Learn More** graphic appears. Click on it to view the course's About page; it should look something like this:

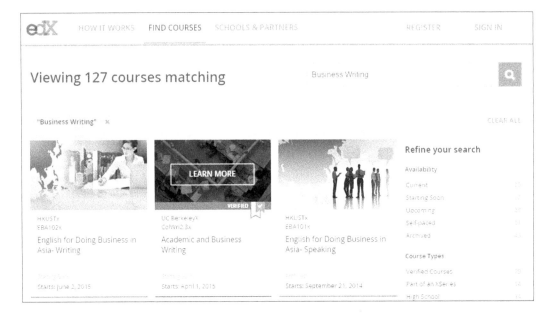

6. Follow the instructions from step 5 in the *Finding courses by navigating* section.

Finding courses by viewing all courses

1. Go to www.edx.org.

2. Click on **VIEW ALL COURSES** under the search box.

3. Follow the instructions from step 3 onwards in the *Finding courses by navigating* section.

Finding courses by home page

1. Go to www.edx.org.

2. Scroll down to view the courses displayed in the **Our Most Popular Courses Starting Soon** section.

3. Follow the instructions from step 3 onwards in the *Finding courses by navigating* section.

Finding courses by refining your search

1. Go to edx.org

2. Click on **COURSES** in the top navigation bar.

3. View the right-hand side of your screen where you will see a column tiled **Refine your search**, like this:

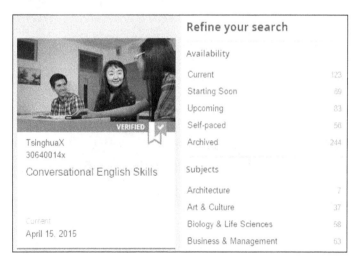

4. Scroll down the page, noting the following categorizations of courses: **Availability, Subjects, Level, Language, Course Types**, and **Schools & Partners**.

5. Click on any of the search terms within each category to refine your search to display only courses that match that criterion.

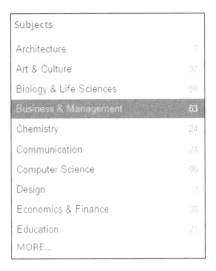

6. Continue refining your search as needed, noting how each selected term is represented in the following screenshot:

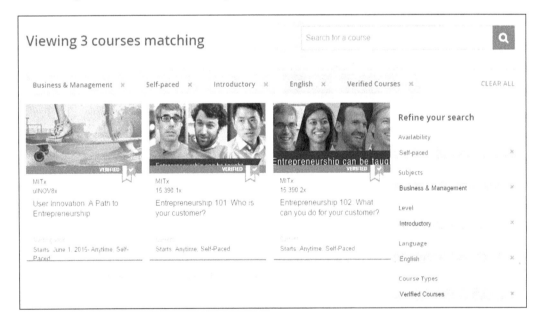

7. Hover over each course until the **Learn More** graphic appears, as shown in the following screenshot. Click on it to view the course's About page.

Signing up for Studio

Studio is the edX authoring tool; think of it as the workshop for your course. You can use Studio to create and integrate your course curriculum with the edX platform, embed links to your instructional YouTube videos, implement exercises and assessments, upload image files and supplemental materials, organize the order of your course materials, and schedule the release dates of your course modules. You can also manage your course team, establish your grading policies, and publish your course.

You can access Studio directly through your web browser; no additional software is needed. As an example, the following is a screenshot of the edX Studio login screen for an edX Edge course:

Instructions for registering an account with Studio and accessing your course are covered in the following sections. There are actually three versions of the edX platform. Whichever version of edX you have access to, you will be able to use Studio to create and manage your courses. Additional details about each edX version are as follows.

edX

The edX website, `edX.org`, is home to the official edX courses, and is widely accessible for student enrollment. Only the faculty of xConsortium member institutions can author courses here (all courses must also be approved).

To publish a course on `edX.org`, you must first have an agreement with edX and an approval from your university. You will author your edX course through `https://studio.edx.org`.

To sign up for Studio on `edX.org`, follow these steps:

1. Complete the registration form at: `https://studio.edx.org/signup`.

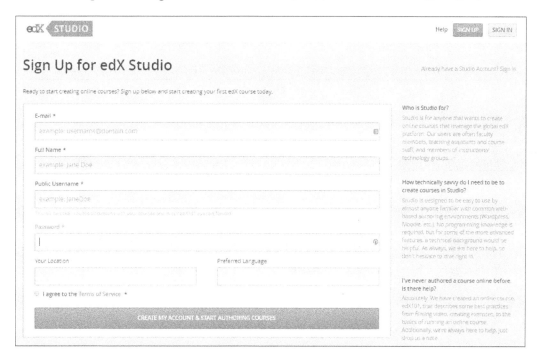

2. Click on the link in the activation e-mail to finish the account creation process.
3. Log in to author your courses at `https://studio.edx.org/signin`.
4. Follow the instructions in the *Creating your course* section later in this chapter.

edX Edge

edX Edge (`https://edge.edx.org/login`) is an alternate option for an xConsortium faculty that wants to publish an edX course in a supported environment without the restrictions and requirements of `edX.org`. edX Edge can also be used to host SPOCs.

It looks similar and functions identically to edX, but there is no catalog of courses, so students will need the URL of your course to register. Courses on edX Edge will not appear on `edX.org`; the two versions are completely separate from each other. Eventually, all courses on `edX.org` will be developed on edX Edge and will then be migrated to `edX.org`.

To sign up for Studio on edX Edge, perform these steps:

1. Complete the registration form at `https://studio.edge.edx.org/signup`.

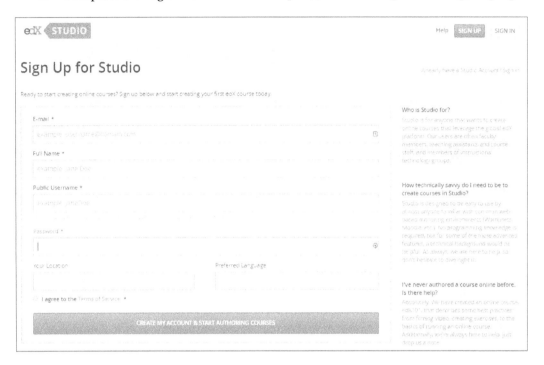

2. Click on the link in the activation e-mail to finish the account creation process.

3. Log in to author your courses at `https://studio.edge.edx.org/signin`.

4. Follow the instructions in the *Creating your course* section later in this chapter.

Open edX

Open edX (`https://open.edx.org`) is the open source version of the edX platform. All of the code you need to install a fully functional version of edX on private servers can be downloaded free of charge here.

This lets institutions host their own instances of Open edX and offer their own MOOC classes. Likewise, educators can extend the platform to build learning tools that precisely meet their needs. Additionally, developers can experiment and contribute new features to the Open edX platform.

The goal in releasing edX in an open source format is to help build a global community that includes educators and technologists. Through their collaborative efforts, innovative approaches and new tools that benefit students everywhere can be created.

Keep in mind, however, that edX requires a high degree of technical ability to install and manage, so you will need a skilled technical team to install and maintain it. The URL for signing up for Studio and accessing it to create courses will vary by installation.

You can review a list of sites powered by Open edX (sorted by the primary course language and then alphabetized) at https://github.com/edx/edx-platform/wiki/Sites-powered-by-Open-edX.

Creating your course

Once you receive a notice saying that you've been approved to create courses, follow these steps:

1. Log in to Studio at https://studio.edx.org (for edX) or https://studio.edge.edx.org (for edX Edge). The URL will vary for the installations of Open edX.

You can experiment with a sandbox installation of edX by logging in to Studio at https://studio.sandbox.edx.org/signin with an e-mail address of staff@example.com and a password of edx. You can also view a live version of the sandbox course at https://www.sandbox.edx.org, using the same log-in credentials as the sandbox studio. See the *Characteristics of your course* section for detailed login instructions.

2. Click on the green **+ Create Your First Course** button.

3. Click on the green **+ New Course** button (for subsequent courses).

4. Enter the course information in the **Create a New Course** form, as shown in the following screenshot:

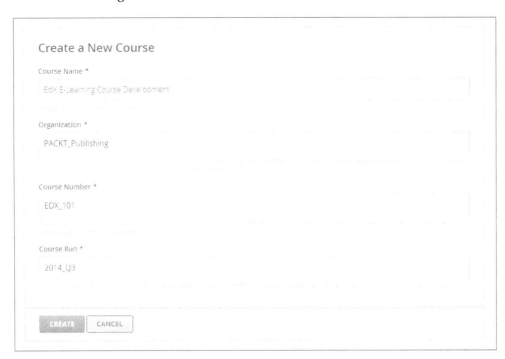

> В_。

Your course information becomes a part of the web address of your course, so enter it carefully. If you are creating your course on edX or edX Edge, you must contact the edX help site (`http://help.edge.edx.org`) to change it. Also keep in mind that the total number of characters in the following fields is limited to 65:

- **Course Name**: Enter the title of your course, using title capitalization.
- **Organization**: Enter the name of your university or company. Do not include whitespace or special characters; use an underscore instead.
- **Course Number**: Enter an abbreviation and a number for the topic and title of your course. In the preceding example, the course was numbered `EDX_101`, which corresponds to EdX Course 101. Do not include whitespaces or special characters here.

 If your course is open to the world, be sure to include the "x" at the end. If it is exclusively an on-campus offering, do not include the "x."

5. Click the blue **Create** button.
6. View your empty course on edX Edge:
   - Click on the blue **View Live** button in the course outline in Studio
   - Log in directly from the edX or edX Edge URL
7. Find the course you just created in the listing of available courses.

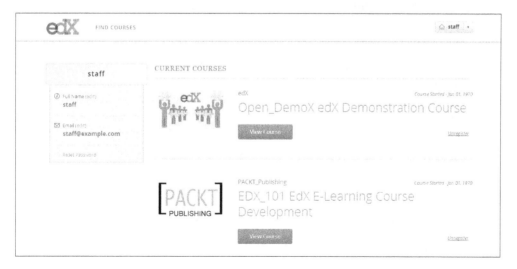

8. Click on the blue **View Course** button to access your course.

Characteristics of your course

Now that you've signed up for Studio and created your first course, let's discuss its characteristics. Although edX is an innovative approach to online learning, you'll find the interface familiar if you've previously taught online. The difference is in the delivery of your course and the potential size of its enrollment.

Your course follows a hierarchical structure, starting with course tabs. Within each tab are sections containing subsections, in which there are units. It is the units in which you will place your actual course components (discussions, HTML, problems, or videos).

When you first create a course, it includes the following tabs by default. As you develop your curriculum, you can add more tabs that align with your learning objectives:

- **Courseware**: Your students spend a significant portion of time accessing your curriculum here. Clicking on the **Courseware** tab reveals all sections of your course and the content in each of them. The **Courseware** tab is always visible in the top-left corner of the page, regardless of any customization. Students can click on it at any time and return to the lesson they were previously viewing.

- **Course Info**: Updates and announcements about your course can be posted here, along with downloadable material in the **Course Handouts** sidebar.

- **Discussion**: All the discussions on a course are accessible via this tab. You and your students can sort them by the date of the most recent comments, the number of votes a thread received, and the number of comments made in a thread.

- **Wiki**: This is a collaborative space where you and your students can freely share ideas. You might also post course updates or known technical issues.

- **Progress**: Students can see how much coursework they've completed and how much remains. Scores for each exercise are posted, along with the number of exercises that are not yet completed.

- **Instructor**: This tab opens the **Instructor** dashboard, which displays administrative tools such as **Course Info**, **Membership**, **Student Admin**, **Data Download**, and **Analytics**.

To help you visualize the potential form and function of your edX course, take a look at the following screenshots from these two edX courses: *edX: Open_DemoX edX Demonstration Course* and *MITx: 8.01x Classical Mechanics*. The first example is from *edX: Open_DemoX edX Demonstration Course*, a functional demo course available on edX's public Studio Sandbox (as introduced before in the *Creating your course* section and further explained later in the *Public Studio Sandbox* subsection).

Your course will likely resemble this when you first start working with it:

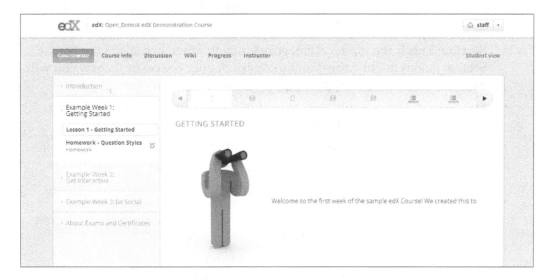

The following screen capture of *MITx: 8.01x Classical Mechanics* serves as an example of a customized edX.org course. Note the additional tabs and how fully developed the content is. Pay careful attention to the learning sequence of instructional videos and exercises displayed across the ribbon above the video in the **Week 1** unit.

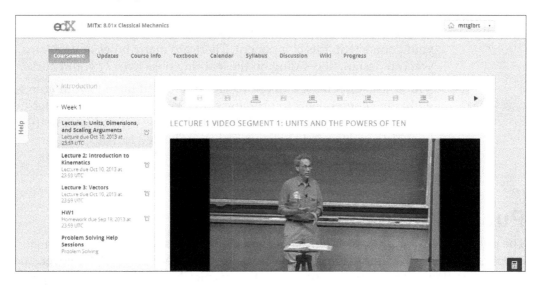

Having reviewed the course tabs and their functions, let's review the structural elements of our course. Unlike the course tabs, these cannot be changed; they are the foundation on which your course is built:

- **Section**: This is the top-level category you will use to organize your course. Section names might correspond to weeks in your course or themes you will explore. Section names appear in the course accordion in the left pane.

- **Subsection**: This is a subcategory within a section, which corresponds to a lesson. Each lesson will contain a mixture of units.

- **Unit**: This is a part of a lesson containing at least one component. A unit is not represented in the course accordion, but appears in the course ribbon at the top of the workspace.

- **Component**: This is the area in a unit containing your course content, represented by an icon in that unit's ribbon. There are four types of content that you can add to your edX course:

  ○ **Discussion**: This is where you and your students add posts, comments, and responses to a question. Discussions in an individual unit appear in the course's discussion forum.

  ○ **HTML**: This is used to add information to a unit, including text, lists, links, and images. You can import LaTeX code here and insert hand-coded content (or content you've programmed using a WYSIWYG editor).

  ○ **Problem**: You can add interactive, automatically graded exercises to your course with this component. There are many types of problems you can design, depending on the learning objectives of your course.

  ○ **Video**: You can create videos of lectures and add them to your course with other components to promote active learning. Adding a video to your course requires several steps that will be defined later in this book. edX is designed to stream videos uploaded to YouTube, but you can also make .mp4 files of every video available for students to download.

Public Studio Sandbox

The public Studio Sandbox is a safe, stable, and standalone space where you can experiment with edX without affecting the actual course. Keep in mind, however, that the Sandbox account can be reset at any time, typically weekly, so any changes you make to it will only be temporary. Also, since it is a public account, anyone can make changes to it at any time.

You can access the public Studio Sandbox using these steps:

1. Go to `https://www.sandbox.edx.org`.
2. Click on the blue **Log in** button.
3. Enter the **E-mail** address as `staff@example.com`.
4. Provide **Password** as **edx**.
5. Log in to `https://studio.sandbox.edx.org` to access Studio for the Sandbox (using the same credentials as mentioned previously).
6. Log in to `https://preview.sandbox.edx.org` to preview your course.

Summary

This chapter introduced edX as both a MOOC platform and an organization, while helping you understand its potential and purpose. We reviewed our role and responsibilities as an edX instructor, discovering best practices in the process.

You were guided through the process of signing up for edX, creating an Studio account, and taking the first steps towards creating your first course. You learned about the characteristics of a typical edX course and were also shown an example of a more customized edX class.

In *Chapter 2*, *Planning the Curriculum*, we will move from ideas to action and begin the curriculum development process. Starting with a Course Matrix—a recommended administrative tool you can use to map your curriculum—we will tackle the tasks necessary to plan and prepare the curriculum for our course.

2
Planning the Curriculum

The previous chapter provided you with an overview of edX as both a MOOC platform and an organization, while helping you understand its potential and purpose. You were also introduced to your role and responsibilities as an edX instructor. Now that you have gained an understanding of edX, signed up for Studio, and launched your first course, let's start planning your curriculum.

This chapter identifies your course's instructional elements and introduces the components of the curriculum that you will create in *Chapter 3, Producing Videos*, and *Chapter 4, Designing Exercises*. We will add these materials into our edX course and review their specific requirements in *Chapter 5, Integrating Curriculum*.

This chapter reviews what you'll need to know, as follows:

- Create your edX Course Matrix
- Prepare your course's About page
- Write preliminary documents
- Understand learning sequences
- Develop exercises and assessments
- Select textbooks and materials
- Moderate the discussion forum
- Launch a Wiki for your course
- Prepare the course certificate

edX Course Matrix

The first step to developing your edX course is organizing its curriculum. Whether you're creating a new course or converting an existing course, you will need to identify each of the components of your course and where they will be delivered to students. While a syllabus was an effective option in the past, you might find it inadequate with the more interactive and engaging elements of your edX course.

While not part of the edX platform, one tool you might find useful is the **edX Course Matrix**. A Microsoft Excel document that outlines the course curriculum with links to the source material and finished files for each instructional element, the edX Course Matrix provides you with a simplified project management process. This document is not required by any means, but it is included here as a value-added best practice.

The following is a screenshot of the edX Course Matrix. As you can see, there are two parts of it: **Course Data** at the top and **Course Details** at the bottom. We will further discuss each part of the edX Course Matrix in the upcoming subsections.

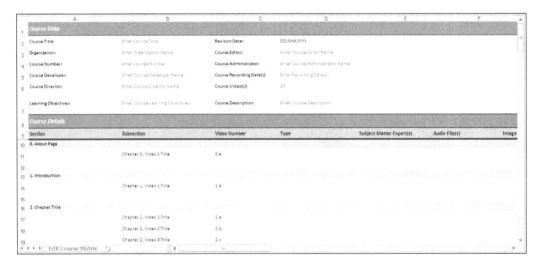

 Download your copy of the edX Course Matrix from this title's book page on the Packt Publishing website at https://www.packtpub.com/hardware-and-creative/edx-e-learning-course-development.

edX Course Matrix data

Let's take a look at the **Course Data** part of the edX Course Matrix, a screenshot of which is provided here:

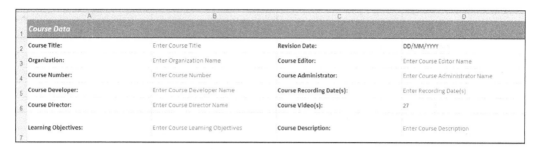

You will notice that three of the fields — **Course Title**, **Organization**, and **Course Number** — mirror the fields you completed when you created your course in the *Creating your course* section in *Chapter 1, Getting Started*. The instructions are repeated in this section for your reference, but the data entered in your Course Matrix should mirror the information you used when creating your course:

- **Course Title**: Enter the title of your course using title capitalization (that is, the first letter of each word must be capitalized).

- **Organization**: Enter the name of your university or company. Do not include whitespaces or special characters; use an underscore between words instead (for example, `Harvard_University`, and not `Harvard University`).

- **Course Number**: Enter an abbreviation and a number for the topic and title of your course. Do not include whitespaces or special characters; use an underscore between words instead. In the preceding example, the course was numbered EDX_101, which corresponds to EdX Course 101.

 Note that, if you want anyone anywhere in the world to be able to enroll in your course, be sure to include "x" in its title. If it is exclusively an on-campus offering, do not include "x".

- **Course Developer**: Enter the name of the lead individual responsible for developing the course.

- **Course Director**: Mention the name of the individual who directed the recording of the educational videos for the course.

- **Learning Objectives**: State the measurable skills or knowledge a learner should have after taking your course. According to Robert F. Mager, PhD, a learning objective should include three components: a measurable verb, the essential condition during which the desired performance should occur, and the criterion of acceptable performance.

- **Revision Date**: Enter the date you last updated your edX Course Matrix to ensure that you are working from the latest version.

  You are encouraged to always save your edX Course Matrix as a new file when you update it, making sure you add the date and/or a version number to the filename. Adding the date in the YYYYMMDD format at the beginning or end of your filename (if the preceding naming of your files is consistent) allows easier sorting of your files. It also ensures that you can easily identify and use the most recent edition of your edX Course Matrix.

- **Course Editor**: Type the name of the video and/or audio editor for the course materials here. Additionally (or alternately), you can state the name of someone who reviewed the course here.

- **Course Administrator**: Enter the name of the person primarily responsible for implementing and administering the technical details of the course.

  - For more information on this aspect of edX, see Packt Publishing's companion publication *EdX Course Administration*

- **Course Recording Date(s)**: Indicate the date (or dates) when the videos were recorded for your course. This is primarily for future reference, but it might also be useful to determine when materials need to be revised.

- **Course Video(s)**: This is an automatically generated field that displays the number of videos in a course. The number is calculated by a simple Excel formula that counts the total number of videos in a course.

  - Click on the cell in which the number count is displayed to see the formula: =COUNTA(C11:C477). This includes section 0 (the About page) through section 10 (the Conclusion). The actual number of sections in your course can vary.

  - The formula counts cells in the range containing text; the range is defined as (C11:C477) in the template, but the range in your document might differ.

- To ensure you are informed only about the number of videos in your course and not the number of every subsection, you have to indicate only the scene numbers for those subsections with videos.

- **Course Description**: Keeping the learning objectives in mind, describe the goals, delivery methods, types of assessments, and instructional methods for your course. Your course description forms the basis of the content that will appear on the About page of your course (see the following section).

edX Course Matrix details

Now let's review the **Course Details** section of our edX Course Matrix, a screenshot of which is provided here:

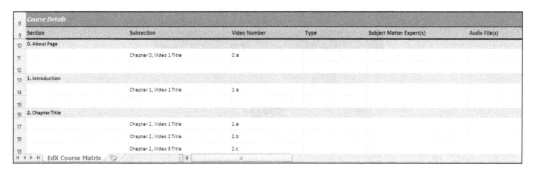

As was the case in the **Course Data** section, the information identified in the **Course Details** section of your edX Course Matrix was previously explained in the *Creating your course* section in *Chapter 1, Getting Started*. However, the information is repeated here for easy reference.

To facilitate your understanding, consider the following screenshot from the *Introduction to Public Speaking* course on `edx.org` as you read through the information after it:

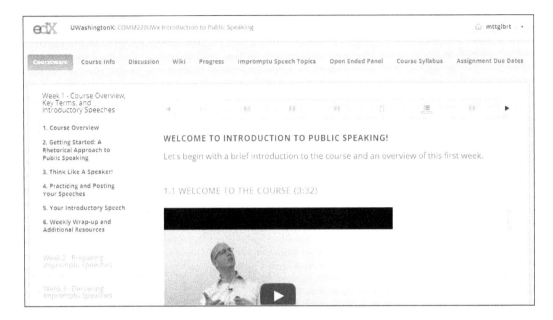

- **Section**: This is the top-level category you will use to organize your course. Section names might correspond to weeks in your course or the themes you will explore. Section names appear in the course accordion in the left pane.

  In the preceding screenshot, the first section is titled *Week 1 - Course Overview, Key Terms, and Introductory Speeches*.

- **Subsection**: This is a subcategory within a section, and it corresponds to a lesson. Each lesson will contain a mixture of units.

  In the preceding screenshot, the first subsection is titled 1 as *Course Overview*. In the edX Course Matrix, you will see suggested subsection numbers of 1.a, 1.b, 1.c, and so on. You can use any scene numbering system that works for your school or organization.

- **Video**: This is the scene number, or some other identifier, of an individual video in your course. You are encouraged to identify videos only based on the section in which they are published and not subsections, because you might have some subsections without videos and others with multiple videos. At the very least, be sure that you have a system for numbering each of your videos so that you can organize and manage them when recording, editing, and integrating them with your course.

In the preceding screenshot, the first video is titled *1.1 WELCOME TO THE COURSE (3:32)*. Note the inclusion of the running time in the video title; this is a helpful piece of information for students, and you are strongly advised to include it.

- **Type**: This column allows you to categorize the content for each subsection using a drop-down menu that is populated with the following default options:
  - ° **Assessment**
  - ° **Audio**
  - ° **PowerPoint**
  - ° **ScreenCap**
  - ° **Text**
  - ° **Video**
  - ° **Other**

- **Subject Matter Expert or Experts**: Identify the individual (or individuals) with advanced knowledge about the subject matter addressed in each video.

- **Audio File or Files**: Include a link (or links) to where the final audio file (or files) can be found for each video.

- **Image File or Files**: Include a link (or links) to where the final image file (or files) can be found for each video.

- **Video File or Files**: Include a link (or links) to where the final video file (or files) can be found for a video; most likely, this will be a YouTube URL.

- **Video Time**: Indicate the runtime of each final produced video file.

- **Video Transcript or Transcripts:** Include a link to where the transcript can be found for a video.

- **Assessment or Assessments**: Include a link (or links) to where the final assessment (or assessments) can be found for a video.

- **Exercise or Exercises**: Include a link (or links) to where the final exercise (or exercises) can be found for a video.

- **Handout or Handouts**: Include a link (or links) to where the final handout (or handouts) can be found for a video.

- **Source Material**: Identify the source material or resources, with or without links, that were used (or could be used) to create the curriculum of your course.

- **Audio Asset or Assets**: Include a link (or links) to where the unedited audio file (or files) can be found for a video.

- **Image Asset or Assets**: Include a link (or links) to where the unedited image file (or files) can be found for a video.

- **Video Asset or assets**: Include a link (or links) to where the unedited video file (or files) can be found for a video.

- **Editing Notes**: Add any notes relevant to the curriculum development and editing process for a video.

Intersecting each of these columns are rows for each section of your course. You will see them numbered from 0 (for the About page) to section 10 (the Conclusion). Note that the About page is not numbered in the edX Course Matrix because it is informative and not instructional in nature. The number of sections will vary by course; you can add them to the edX Course Matrix additional sections or delete those you do not need.

The About page

Your course's About page provides prospective students with information so that they can decide whether they want to enroll. Refer to the *Exploring edX courses* section of *Chapter 1, Getting Started,* to review the various ways to navigate to the About pages for currently available courses.

Consider the following screenshot from the About page for MITx course **uINOV8x**, *User Innovation: A Path to Entrepreneurship*.

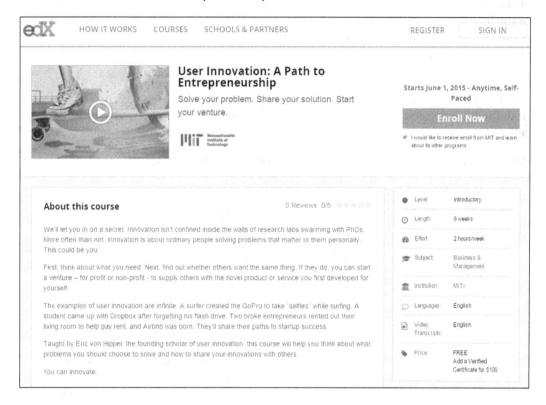

 Remember that, since edX is a cloud-based learning management system, its form and function are always in a state of evolution; the interface or operations could change at any time.

About pages across edX versions

The *Academic and Business Writing* course is available on edX.org; the About page for courses on edX Edge looks similar, but there is no course catalog, so you will need to share the link to the course directly with students. Open edX courses also have an About page, which can be accessed from a course catalog page, similar to that of an edX.org course.

Long course descriptions

Similar to text in a typical printed course catalog, the long course description is one of the first things a prospective student sees about your course. It should ideally be between 150 and 300 words; think of it as a summarized syllabus. In fact, you might even consider using, or at last starting with, your course description from your syllabus.

Be as specific as possible. Outline the topics and skills the course covers, and also how the knowledge gained from the course can be applied to the real world. In short, sell your course.

Address the questions an adult learner might ask, such as these:

- What type of homework assignments, if any, will there be?
- On which days of the week are assignments typically due?
- What types of assessments are there and how many of each?
- How much time should I expect to spend on this class each week?
- In what ways can I apply this class to my professional responsibilities?

You should also identify the preferred method by which, and the specific circumstances under which, students can contact you and/or your course staff. Given the potentially large size of enrollment in your class, you might find it overwhelming to provide a means of direct contact, such as an e-mail address, although using an e-mail address specifically for each course is one way to manage the workflow. You might find it more feasible to direct your students to a specific discussion thread that you monitor actively.

In the following screenshot of the About page of **uINOV8x**, *User Innovation: A Path to Entrepreneurship,* the long course description can be found after the **About this Course** headline.

About this course   0 Reviews 0/5 ⭐☆☆☆☆

We'll let you in on a secret. Innovation isn't confined inside the walls of research labs swarming with PhDs. More often than not, innovation is about ordinary people solving problems that matter to them personally. This could be you.

First, think about what you need. Next, find out whether others want the same thing. If they do, you can start a venture – for profit or non-profit - to supply others with the novel product or service you first developed for yourself.

The examples of user innovation are infinite. A surfer created the GoPro to take "selfies" while surfing. A student came up with Dropbox after forgetting his flash drive. Two broke entrepreneurs rented out their living room to help pay rent, and Airbnb was born. They'll share their paths to startup success.

Taught by Eric von Hippel, the founding scholar of user innovation, this course will help you think about what problems you should choose to solve and how to share your innovations with others.

You can innovate.

Short course descriptions

Think of your short course description as the advertising slogan for your course. Make it equally informative and engaging. You will likely find it easier to write your long course description first and use it as foundation for the short course description. Your short course description must be no longer than 25 words. Let's look again at **uINOV8x**, *User Innovation: A Path to Entrepreneurship,* for an example of a short course description, as shown in the following screenshot:

 A short course description should be equally informative and engaging.

Solve your problem. Share your solution. Start your venture.

Staff biographies

Despite the technological method of course delivery, students generally still want to know who is "behind the curtain" of their edX course. Biographies, titles, and photos of instructors and staff serve that purpose.

Other than the title and qualifications of each staff member, biographies should also offer insights into the personality and teaching philosophies of the people involved in the course. Share something unique about each individual and have some fun doing it. Biographies should be 75 to 100 words long. Pictures should be posed against a solid, non-distracting background, at least 110 x 110 pixels in size, and compressed into a file of size less than 200 kB.

Here are the professional, yet playful, bios (and pictures) of the staff members of **HarvardX: CS50x** *Introduction to Computer Science*. Although brief, these bios are effective, especially since there are several staff members for this course. Likewise, the pictures are friendly and welcoming.

Course Staff

David J. Malan

David is Gordon McKay Professor of the Practice of Computer Science at the School of Engineering and Applied Sciences at Harvard University. He received his A.B., S.M., and Ph.D. in Computer Science from Harvard in 1999, 2004, and 2007, respectively.

Rob Bowden

Rob is a doctoral student in Computer Science at the School of Engineering and Applied Sciences at Harvard University. He received his A.B. in Computer Science with a secondary field in Mathematical Sciences from Harvard in 2013.

Zamyla Chan

Zamyla is a doctoral student in Chemistry and Chemical Biology at the Graduate School of Arts and Sciences at Harvard University. She received her A.B. in Engineering Sciences with a secondary field in Computer Science from Harvard in 2014.

Allison Buchholtz-Au

Allison is an undergraduate student at Harvard College. She will receive her A.B. in Computer Science with a secondary field in Mathematical Sciences from Harvard in 2015.

Compare these examples with the longer biography for the UWashingtonX course **COMM220x_2**, *Introduction to Public Speaking*, as shown in the following screenshot. Both the biography and the picture are more professional in nature, and also communicate professionalism and expertise. Just as your course and you are unique, their reflection in your biography and photo should be as well. Ultimately, write a biography and use a picture that works best for you and the course you are teaching.

Course Staff

Matt McGarrity

Dr. Matt McGarrity is a Senior Lecturer in the Communication Department at the University of Washington. He teaches undergraduate and graduate courses in public speaking, argumentation, classical rhetoric, rhetorical criticism, and communication pedagogy. He founded and continues to direct the University of Washington Speaking Center, which offers speech coaching to students. He has published academic articles and teaching materials on communication education and public speaking and has won multiple top paper awards for public speaking research at academic conferences. He has won a number of teaching awards, including the National Speakers' Association's Outstanding Professor Award.

The alternative About page offers a different, two-part approach to the course staff bios. On **ColWri2.3x**, *Academic and Business Writing*, you will first see a subsection titled **Meet the Instructor**, with a profile picture and the instructor's name; it's under the course learning objectives, which are in a subsection titled **What you'll learn** as shown in this screenshot:

What you'll learn

- Gain an understanding of writing for science & technology, literature, and the social sciences
- Learn to write statements of purpose and develop a professional writing style

Meet the instructor

Maggie Sokolik

After you click on the instructor's picture or name, a profile page displays the full bio, as shown in the following screenshot. If that instructor has taught other courses for edX, you will see them listed at the bottom of the page.

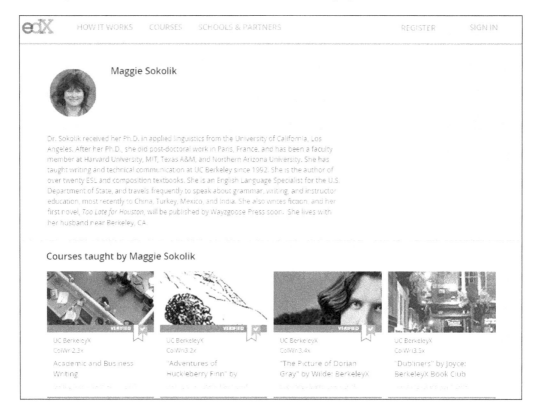

If a course's About page doesn't link to the instructor profile page, you can go to the page for any instructor by entering a link using this format in your web browser: `https://www.edx.org/bio/firstname-lastname`.

Prerequisites

If an edX course has prerequisites, they will typically be displayed in the sidebar on the right side of the About page. You will likely also find them below the course staff bios. For edX Edge courses, the sidebar will indicate whether there are prerequisites. Text describing the details will show up in a **Prerequisites** section.

If there are no academic prerequisites, you can indicate technical requirements for your course, as is done for **COMM220x_2**, *Introduction to Public Speaking*, which is shown in the following screenshot. You will find it in the bottom right hand corner of the About page, under the **Share this course with a friend** icon.

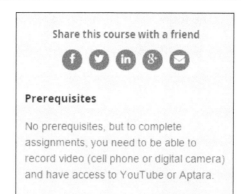

Be specific when writing the prerequisites for your course; it's better to be too detailed than too general. For example, instead of writing Able to use Microsoft Word, write Able to use Microsoft Word 2013. This might appear to be a minor difference, but it is especially important when your course requires knowledge of specific versions of software.

If your course doesn't have prerequisites, indicate that, as is the case with **uINOV8x,** *User Innovation: A Path to Entrepreneurship*. When a course does not have prerequisites, no information will appear where the prerequisite are normally included.

In some circumstances, experience with a free or open source version of a paid software platform might be reasonably considered as a satisfying prerequisite.

Frequently Asked Questions

A **Frequently Asked Questions (FAQ)** section anticipates and addresses the common student questions. Creating an **FAQ** section might reduce the number of inquiries from students – or you could direct students with common questions to your **FAQ** section (see the *Long course descriptions* section earlier in this chapter).

Keep in mind that edX maintains a robust FAQ page on its main site, covering general questions at https://www.edx.org/student-faq. Common FAQs include the following:

- Are there any special system requirements?
- Is there a proctored test?
- Is there a required textbook for the course?
- Is there any special software needed?
- On what day of the week are assignments due?

For reference, take a look at the following **FAQs** from **DelftX: TW3421x**: *An Introduction to Credit Risk Management*. Note how answers to each question are revealed when selected, but are hidden when not active.

```
FAQs

  ▼  What is the estimated effort for course?

     About 6 hrs/week


  ▶  How much does it cost to take the course?

  ▶  Will the text of the lectures be available?

  ▶  Do I need to watch the lectures live?

  ▶  Will certificates be awarded?

  ▶  Can I contact the Instructor or Teaching Assistants?

  ▶  Is this course related to campus courses of Delft University of Technology?
```

Course image

You will need a Course Image for your course; it is similar to the logo of a product or service. The course image appears in the dashboard. Select an image that is eye-catching, but also representative of the course's curriculum and reflective of the environment you want to create in the class. Keep these best practices in mind:

- Avoid using text or headlines; they could get obscured or otherwise be too hard to read
- Make sure it is 378 pixels in width by 225 pixels in height
- Hire a professional photographer or designer to create your descriptive picture

Save your course picture in .jpg or .png formats only. As an example, here is the descriptive picture for **uINOV8x**, *User Innovation: A Path to Entrepreneurship*:

To add your image under Course Image, perform these steps:

1. Select **Schedule & Details** from the **Settings** menu, as shown here:

2. Then, scroll down to the **Course Image** section.

3. Select an image from your computer by clicking on the **Upload Course Image** button (which will turn blue), like this:

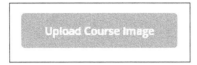

4. Then, follow the prompts to find and upload your image.

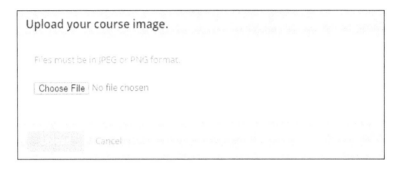

5. Click on the yellow **Save Changes** button that appears at the bottom-right corner of the page, as shown here:

6. Finally, view your dashboard to see how the image will appear to learners in their list of **Current Courses**.

 The course image you add to edX.org in Studio is used on the Learner Dashboard of **Current Courses**, but it won't automatically appear on the course's About page. Work directly with your edX program manager to set up the About page's assets and then the course image for the course' Summary page.

About videos

The About video is like a movie trailer; accordingly, it should be short, but also engaging and informative. In 3 minutes or less your movie should:

- Define what a student should be able to do after the course

- Describe the course's purpose and learning objectives

- Explain why students should take the course

- Introduce the instructor and each staff member

- Give an idea about the style of the course

- Outline why this subject matter is important

- Present the learning objectives

All About videos usually appear in the top-left hand corner of a course's About page, as is the case in the following example from **uINOV8x**, *User Innovation: A Path to Entrepreneurship*:

User Innovation: A Path to Entrepreneurship

Solve your problem. Share your solution. Start your venture.

Massachusetts Institute of Technology

However, there might be variations in the placement of the About video, as is the case with **ColWri2.3x**, *Academic and Business Writing*. This alternative interface design is likely the result of the course being offered at any time as a self-paced class, as opposed to only at specific dates:

About videos are typically YouTube videos embedded in the course's About page. To watch them, simply click on the play icon in the video thumbnail. You can also click on the title of the video once it starts playing on the About page and watch it directly on the YouTube page. You might find it helpful to create playlists on YouTube for each course so that you can watch (and rewatch) the course videos outside edX as desired.

To add your **About Video**, perform these steps:

1. Upload the course video to YouTube and set the privacy setting to **Unlisted**.

 Make a note of the code that appears between watch?v= and &feature in the URL.

2. Select **Schedule & Details** from the **Settings** menu, like this:

3. Then, scroll down to the **Course Introduction Video** section, as shown here:

4. Enter the YouTube video ID (the code you copied in step 1) in the field below the video box. When you add the code, the video will automatically load in the video box.

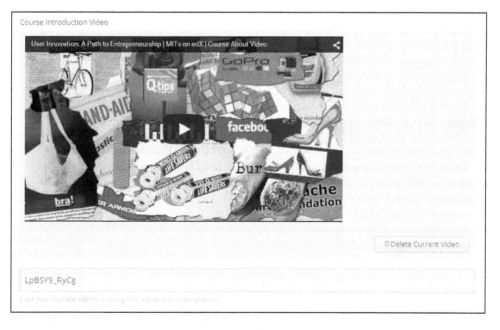

5. Click on the yellow **Save Changes** button that appears at the bottom-right corner of the page, like this:

6. View your course's About page to test how the video will appear to the learners.

 When creating a course for edX.org, you will be working directly with your program manager to set up the course video in the Summary page.

Other course information

Besides the information in the body of the About page, there is additional information in the sidebar on the right-hand side of the page. Consider the following example from uINOV8x, *User Innovation: A Path to Entrepreneurship*:

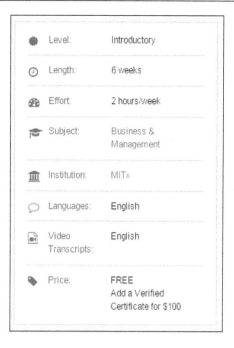

✹	Level:	Introductory
⏱	Length:	6 weeks
⚖	Effort:	2 hours/week
🎓	Subject:	Business & Management
🏛	Institution:	MITx
💬	Languages:	English
🎬	Video Transcripts:	English
🏷	Price:	FREE Add a Verified Certificate for $100

Let's now review each component in this version:

- **Level**: The degree of the course's difficulty.
- **Length**: The number of weeks your course is scheduled to run for.
- **Effort**: The number of hours per week you would expect an average student at your university to spend on your course.

 This is technically an optional field, but this information is especially relevant for working adults who need to determine how feasible taking the course is given their other responsibilities.

- **Subjects**: The academic areas into which the course is categorized. Clicking on any of these links takes you to a list of courses that are similarly categorized.
- **Institution**: Automatically extracted from the information you entered when you first created the course creation information.
- **Languages**: The language (or languages) in which the course curriculum is prepared.

- **Video Transcripts**: The language (or languages) in which the course video transcripts are prepared.

- **Price**: The cost to enroll in the course. This will indicate **Free** or the cost to purchase a verified completion certificate for it.

Preliminary documents

Preliminary documents include an array of instructional materials a student sees when first entering your edX course. Typically, preliminary documents are accessible via the **Course Info** tab, as shown in the following screenshot from the HarvardX course **CS50x**, *Introduction to Computer Science*:

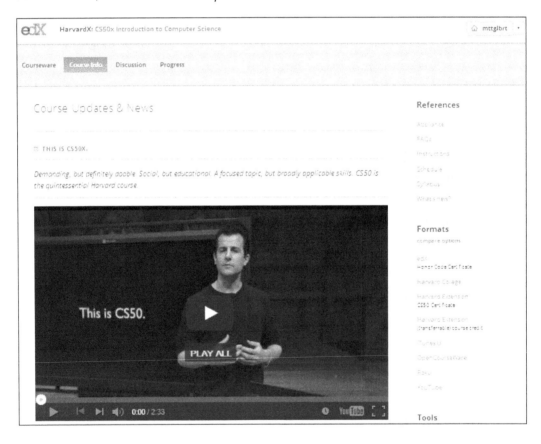

The preliminary documents required for your edX course will vary, based on its learning objectives and requirements, but might generally include the following:

- **Syllabus**: The syllabus should define topics your course will cover, include the names of instructors and teaching assistants, present any grading rubrics, list textbook information, give an overview of assignments and assessments, identify important dates, and define special instructions or policies. Typically, courses offer a syllabus within the edX environment as a downloadable PDF file and/or through an external website.

- **Schedule**: Your schedule defines the order and deadlines for the assignments in your course. There are two ways to create a schedule: by linking a Google Calendar to your course, or with a dynamic HTML schedule. Whichever you chose, remember that your students are engaging your course asynchronously and online from a number of countries. Given that, it is strongly recommended that you go with the Google Calendar option. Specific tips will be provided to help you with this in *Chapter 5, Integrating the Curriculum*.

- **Discussion Guidelines**: You will need to outline your expectations for each discussion question in your course: how many posts are required, how many times a student needs to reply to a classmate, and more. You should also address etiquette, best practices, and formatting. You could let students know when forum moderators will be online and available for questions.

- **Announcements and Email Messages**: Creating a positive first impression while making your students feel comfortable in your class can be achieved through a well-worded welcome announcement. Likewise, you should craft complete and clear weekly announcements and e-mail messages that outline what is happening, when assignments are due, and what is expected from your students that week. Remember that you want to be professional, but you should also endeavor to be personable in your messages.

If you're curious to see the schedule of an actual edX course, take a look at the Google Calendar for BerkeleyX's **CS-169.1x**, *Software as a Service*:

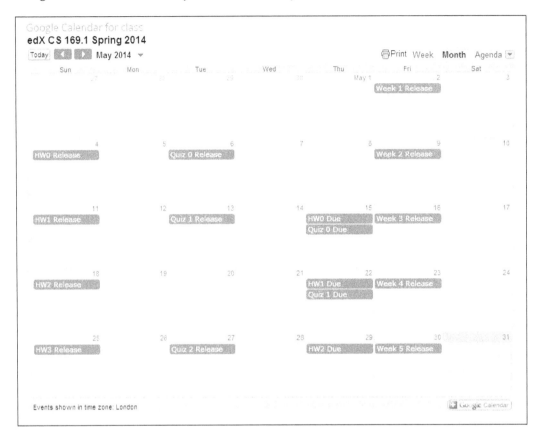

Learning sequences

The backbone of the educational experience in edX is the learning sequence. Inspired by the Socratic method, this is a novel approach to instruction by which you interweave exercises and a video lecture sequence (typically, short assessments with one to five questions each). Think of a learning sequence as a longer lecture that is broken down into smaller parts.

Each learning sequence appears within your course's weekly courseware sections, which are called modules, weeks, or sometimes hours. In each section, you can place homework, tutorials, and a virtual laboratory environment, if relevant. For reference, **Module 1** from **BUx: SABR101x**, *Sabermetrics 101: Introduction to Baseball Analytics* is shown here:

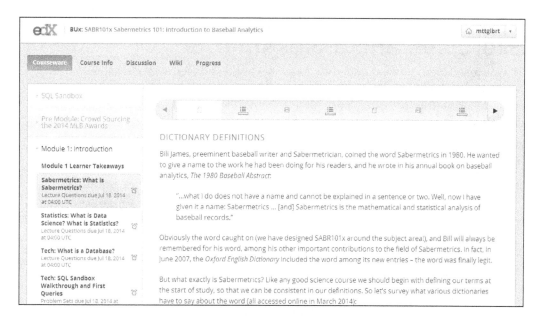

In the preceding screenshot, we are in **Sabermetrics: What is Sabermetrics?**. This is the second subsection within this course's first section, **Module 1: Introduction**.

There are seven icons—one for each unit in this subsection—that represent a combination of written lecture notes, quizzes, video lectures, and discussion forums. Collectively, these comprise the learning sequence for this subsection. A closer look at this navigational bar reveals some of the details for each unit, as shown in this screenshot:

When developing the curriculum for your edX course, keep in mind that the goal is active learning: your students should be participating in your course content more often than passively observing it, as is the case with a traditional classroom lecture. Remain mindful of this important distinction; it's better to have a larger quantity of units that are shorter than fewer units crammed with more content.

Exercises and assessments

As was just noted, you will need to create several exercises and assessments for your course. Typically, these are short-answer or multiple-choice quizzes that are sandwiched within the other parts of a learning sequence. However, there are actually four types of exercises you can create for your course:

- **In-lesson exercises**: Designed as short knowledge checks within a learning sequence, in-lesson exercises should focus on one or two small ideas. They should be challenging enough to ensure that a student understands the material, but not so intense that they break the rhythm of the course. In-lesson exercises can be used for instruction, feedback, and assessment.

- **Homework questions**: These should ask more in-depth questions that link several course concepts and require more critical thinking than an in-lesson exercise. Consider developing homework questions as a weekly wrap-up.

- **Quiz problems**: Whereas in-lesson exercises assess knowledge within a learning sequence, quiz problems are short-graded exercises your students can take to review their knowledge of a section or help prepare for exams.

- **Exam problems**: You can develop exam problems to assess your students' mastery of a specific section of your course once they've completed all the learning sequences it contains. Typically, exams are offered during a fixed time and have a short time limit. You can turn off discussion forums when exams are offered to increase their difficulty.

To better understand the assessment options you just saw, view the following screenshots of the **Lesson 1 Quiz** from **BerkleeX: BMPR365x,** *Vocal Recording Technology*. The first screenshot shows the question before the answer is checked or saved:

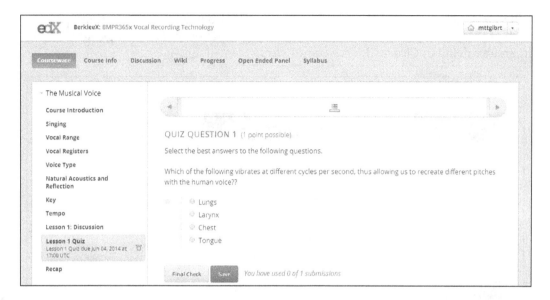

The second screenshot shows the same question after the answer was submitted, along with an explanation that supports the correct answer. As you develop the exercises and assessments, you will need to prepare explanations corresponding to the correct answers to help your students better understand the course's content.

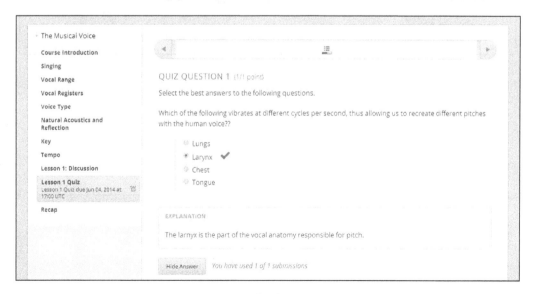

Finally, as a point of reference for the preceding **Lesson 1 Quiz** screenshots, see the following screenshot of the Lesson 1 video about singing; it is at this point in the video that the answer to the question appears (note the bold portion of the video transcript).

When producing videos for your course, you will also need to prepare transcripts for each of them to facilitate your students' learning experience. This will be addressed in greater detail in *Chapter 3, Producing Videos*.

Textbooks and course materials

In the past you likely required your students to purchase a physical textbook, a course reader, and, in some cases, an eBook. However, the textbook for your edX course must be made available for free in an electronic format. You have three options when it comes to the textbook for your edX course:

- **Provide a free digital textbook**: You will need to work with the publisher to license and create a free digital copy of the textbook. Due to the complex nature of this process, you should start it with your program manager as soon as possible.

- **Use freely available textbooks**: There is an impressive selection of digital books, peer-reviewed articles, educational media, and instructional material available at no cost from learning object repositories. Options include:

    ° Connexions (Rice University): `http://cnx.org`

    ° Creative Commons: `http://creativecommons.org/`

    ° Google Books: `http://books.google.com`

    ° LibriVox: `https://librivox.org`

    ° Merlot (California State University): `http://www.merlot.org`

    ° Open Educational Resource Commons: `http://www.oercommons.org`

    ° Open Culture: `http://www.openculture.com`

    ° Project Gutenberg: `http://www.gutenberg.org`

    ° The Online Books Page (University of Pennsylvania): `http://onlinebooks.library.upenn.edu`

    ° Wikibooks: `http://wikibooks.org`

- **Collaborate with a librarian**: If none of the preceding options results in your finding a textbook, or if you want to add more material to enhance your students' experience, discuss your needs with your institution's librarian. As an expert in copyright law and library science, a librarian can help you identify options that might match your needs.

One admirable approach to providing students with a textbook can be found in BerkleeX **MB110x**, *Introduction to the Music Business*. Students provided a link in an announcement in the **Course Info** section of the class to download a free **Music Business Handbook**. The link then goes to a form hosted on the website of Berklee College of Music.

Discussion forums

If you've previously taught online, you will be well aware of the importance of your course's discussion forum to the success rate of its students.

One way to encourage interaction in your edX course is to develop discussion questions that are engaging and invite students to share their personal or professional stories, along with their opinions. Look for ways to integrate the discussion questions with your learning sequences, or encourage engagement.

In addition, you and/or a staff member of your course will need to moderate the forum to make sure students' questions are answered, issues are addressed, and engagement is kept at a high level. You might also consider inviting some students who are doing well in the course to serve as moderators, especially if you have a large enrollment and find it challenging to manage the volume and speed of response in the forum.

One creative way to produce written resource material for your course is to ask students to collaboratively create lecture notes for the course. You could create a special forum in the **Discussions** where students can add their notes, which you can curate and prepare.

For your reference, consider this screenshot of the Discussion Forum from BerkleeX: **BMPR365x**, *Vocal Recording Technology*:

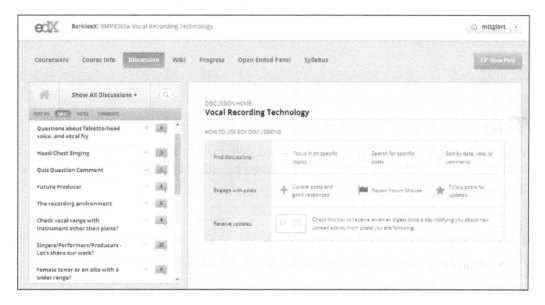

The course Wiki

Every edX course provides **Wiki** functionality; you can use it in whatever manner you feel best suits your course and the needs of your students. Some common ways the **Wiki** has been used include the following:

- Archive of websites referenced in a class
- Links to student-developed resources
- Online errata and technical issues
- Suggestions for course changes
- User-editable course handouts

Here's a screenshot showing the **Wiki** from **CaltechX: Ay1001x**, *The Evolving Universe*:

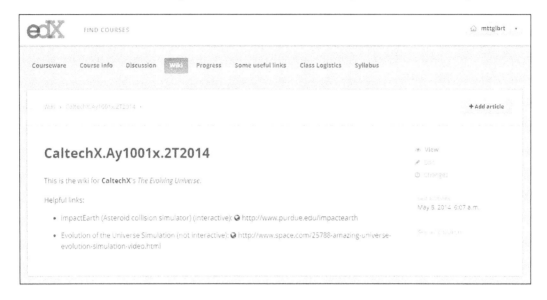

The course certificate

When students successfully complete your edX course, they will receive a Certificate of Mastery. Certificates are automatically issued by edX, but you will need to provide:

- The preferred spelling of your name
- Your official title
- A high-resolution scan of your signature
- The certificate issue date (which must be after the last due date)

The Certificate of Mastery for your course will resemble the sample shown in the following screenshot:

Summary

This chapter focused on planning the curriculum for your course and explaining the elements within edX necessary for launching it.

You were introduced to the edX Course Matrix. You learned how to prepare your course's About page, write the various preliminary documents for your course, improve your knowledge of learning sequences, design exercises and assessments, choose textbooks and materials, moderate the discussion forum, and launch your course's Wiki. You also previewed the necessary information for the Certificate of Mastery for your course.

In *Chapter 3, Producing Videos*, we will take the first steps to actually creating our curriculum as we venture into video production. You will understand instructional videos, learn video production pointers, preview post-production processes, review creating video transcripts, and discuss YouTube best practices.

3
Producing Videos

If video killed the radio star, will it do the same to traditional classroom lectures?

With its first broadcast on August 1, 1981, MTV ushered in a new era of entertainment with the song "Video Killed the Radio Star" as the standard bearer. Likewise, the emergence of edX along with Coursera, MIT's OpenCourseWare, Udacity, and other early-entry MOOCs set a new standard in scholarship by converting classroom lectures into online instructional videos.

Interestingly, the evolution of education from an on-campus experience to an online environment parallels cultural trends such as that of television, where viewership is rapidly migrating away from traditional providers to online options. People prefer watching Netflix to network shows, streaming Hulu instead of watching shows according to a schedule, and spending hours watching YouTube from the convenience of their mobile devices.

In a victory for "cord cutters", cable television network HBO launched HBO NOW, a streaming-only subscription service in 2015. Previously, HBO had offered HBO GO, a streaming service cable or satellite that subscribers can use to watch HBO's programs on mobile devices or the Web. There is no need for a subscription with HBO NOW. Your students reflect this reality: they want to consume your curriculum on their laptops and mobile devices according to their schedule—not yours. Fortunately, you don't have to be a rock star to produce instructional videos but, with a modest investment of time and resources, you can create compelling content. We'll focus on the practical aspects of video production in this chapter and carry out the following activities:

- Understanding instructional videos
- Learning video production pointers
- Previewing post-production processes
- Reviewing the creation of video transcripts
- Discussing YouTube best practices

Instructional videos

As MOOCs have hit critical mass, the use of online instructional videos has accordingly skyrocketed. This isn't surprising when you compare the high cost of traditional higher education with the highly cost-effective nature of MOOCs.

According to Coursera, co-founder Daphne Koller shared in her 2012 TED Talk *What We're Learning from Online Education*, tuition at institutions of higher education has increased an astonishing 559% during the previous 25 years!

 Watch Koller's TED Talk *What We're Learning from Online Education* at `http://www.ted.com/talks/daphne_koller_what_we_re_learning_from_online_education`.

Your instructional videos enable you to share your knowledge with a wider audience, achieving one goal of edX to "expand access to education for everyone". Likewise, your videos "enhance teaching and learning on campus and online" — another edX goal.

Creating the most effective educational videos requires you to understand and embrace best practices and industry benchmarks. Certainly, the medium is dynamic and it continues to evolve, but you need to follow the current guidelines for this:

- **Answer the "why"**: Highlight the real-world implications of your lesson; this reinforces your message and puts it into perspective for your audience.

- **Clean your desktop**: For screen capture videos, hide unnecessary taskbars, quit any irrelevant applications, hide the clock, deactivate any reminders that might pop up during recording. If you are demonstrating a piece of software or an online application, create a clean user account without personal data.

- **Engage your audience**: Speak in plain, clear terms while making sure to define unfamiliar terms the first time you use them.

- **Establish a goal**: First tell your audience what you're going to teach them, teach them the lesson, and review what you just taught. Show your students the desired final product — their goal — at the beginning of your video.

- **Keep it short**: Each video should be between three and six minutes long. If you go beyond this length, consider breaking your video into shorter parts. An edX blog post titled *Optimal Video Length for Student Engagement* supports this idea. Author Philip Guo, an assistant professor of Computer Science at the University of Rochester whose research interests are in human-computer interaction and online education, writes: "The optimal video length is 6 minutes or shorter… the average engagement time of any video maxes out at 6 minutes, regardless of its length. And engagement times decrease as videos lengthen".

 Read Philip Guo's blog post *Optimal Video Length for Student Engagement* and view his related research online at https://www.edx.org/blog/optimal-video-length-student-engagement.

- **Pay attention to your setting**: Remove any clutter and ideally shoot in front of a solid background or a Chroma key (this is especially important if you plan to add a virtual background during post-production). You can alternately shoot in front of a whiteboard, chalkboard, or neutral classroom setting.

- **Outline your video**: You don't always need to write a script; instead script the introduction and the conclusion while using bullet points for the content.

- **Practice your lines**: Practice delivering your script to avoid sounding too stiff; you want to develop a natural rhythm and sound conversational when you record your video. The more you practice, the more natural your delivery will be on camera.

- **Rephrase your mistakes**: Making a mistake is inevitable. So, when you do make an error, simply stop, pause, and say "rephrase". This will act as a signal to whoever will be editing your video in post-production.

- **Share your personality**: Don't change your personality or act in a certain way; that is not how you typically teach but just be yourself! Let your enthusiasm for the subject show through your work along with making sure you stay as focused and professional as possible. Your video should be engaging.

For additional instructional video production tips, review the following resources:

- Creative Live: *Micro Budget Filmmaking - The Art of Filmmaking and Editing* at `https://youtu.be/T04VB6NDKaA`

- Edutopia: *MOOCing It: 10 Tips for Creating Compelling Video Content* at `http://www.edutopia.org/blog/mooc-create-compelling-video-content-ainissa-ramirez`

- *edX101 Overview of Creating an edX Course | Phase 2: Creating Course Content | Creating Video* at `https://courses.edx.org/courses/edX/edX101/2014/courseware/c2a1714627a945afaceabdfb651088cf/9dd6e5fdf64b49a89feac208ab544760/`

- Flipped Learning: *Making Quality Flipped Class Videos* at `http://flipped-learning.com/?p=1176`

- Florida Institute of Technology: *How to Prepare for a Video Recording Session* at `http://it.fit.edu/instructional/video_prep.php`

- HarvardX Techops Studio 125 at `https://vimeo.com/114275512`

- `Lynda.com`: *Video Production Techniques: Promotional Videos* (Subscription Required) at `http://www.lynda.com/Video-Shooting-Video-tutorials/Video-Production-Techniques-Promotional-Videos/129012-2.html`

- Purdue University Instructional Development Center Blog: *Tips for Creating Instructional Videos* at `https://www.purdue.edu/learning/blog/?p=6696`

- UC Berkeley Educational Technology Services: *Resources and Tutorials for Video Production* at `http://ets.berkeley.edu/help/resources-and-tutorials-video-production-0`

- Videomaker: *How to Videos - 10 Tips to Make More Effective Training Videos* at `http://www.videomaker.com/videonews/2012/10/how-to-videos-10-tips-to-making-more-effective-training-videos`

- Vimeo Video School at `https://vimeo.com/videoschool`

- Wistia Library at `http://wistia.com/library`

This information should give you a good grasp of what's necessary to create engaging and effective instructional videos for your edX course. In the next section, we will share video production pointers and best practices.

Video production pointers

When you begin to produce videos for your course, the first thing to understand is that there are two main approaches to recording them:

- **Screen recording**: This method is most useful to teach software programs or export PowerPoint presentations; these videos allow a student to follow along as you demonstrate a piece of software using your computer or tablet. To enhance the quality of these videos, many instructors adopt a picture-in-picture approach that features them talking while the main portion of the screen displays the software being demonstrated. They are typically simpler to record and often easier to edit.

- **Live action**: These videos require an individual to stand in front of a camera and speak to the camera. You can also add on-screen graphics to complement the spoken words of the instructor and to visually illustrate concepts. These require the most preparation and post-production work, but they are highly engaging. These are typically recorded in a studio, but can also be recorded during one of your regular classroom lectures with students present, but you might lose significant control of your surroundings.

Seven video production strategies

While creating screen recording videos takes some practice, recording a live action video requires more effort, equipment, and expertise. To help you understand the process, we turn to advice from an expert named Dominique Samario.

More than a decade of experience producing videos gives Dominique exceptional insight into best practices and tricks of the trade. In addition to working as an administrative analyst and public information officer for the city of Santa Barbara Waterfront Department, she manages Dominique Samario Media & Communications.

Speaking to those new to the craft, Dominique clarifies that "creating quality instructional videos doesn't require years of specialized training or thousands of dollars in equipment, but it does take preplanning and patience".

To help you improve your video production preplanning process, Dominique has shared the following seven key video production strategies. Once you understand her insights, put them into practice with a few test takes until you are ready to record the real thing.

The seven video production strategies are:

1. **Realize that great production starts in pre-production**: Recording a high-quality video begins during your pre-production planning process. Having a thorough outline of what you plan to cover and what you would like to show visually for each shot is a critical step in making sure you have the footage you need when you finish filming and start the editing process. Although it requires additional time and effort, completing the organizational and scripting work prior to shooting your video will save you time. That said, it's important to remain flexible and open to improvisation as the relevant opportunities arise; you might find that the best parts of your videos were those that occurred in an impromptu way.

 Read scripting tips from Wistia—a provider of professional video hosting with viewer analytics, HD video delivery, and marketing tools—in its user library article *Wistia's Scripting Tips* at http:// wistia.com/library/wistia-s-scripting-tips.

2. **Understand that equipment doesn't have to be expensive**: Expensive gear does not guarantee a good video nor does inexpensive equipment doom you to failure, but it's quite the opposite. You can create a professional video without investing thousands of dollars in equipment. Start with a high-definition (HD) recording device that records video in a digital format either on a solid-state drive (SSD) or a secure digital (SD) memory card. This will make the footage transfer process faster and simpler. Even consumer-grade camcorders, which you can find for less than $1,000, record very good-quality video. However, beware of popular DSLR cameras; while they shoot beautiful footage and there are several options available at the lower end of the price scale, they require a high degree of skill. Know what you are getting into before purchasing; reviewing technology websites and speaking with professional video stores can help you to understand your options and make the right decision.

Learn about setting up a video recording studio in the Wistia article *DIY Office Video Studio* available at `http://wistia.com/library/diy-office-video-studio` and evaluate equipment options via the website *Equipment for low budget filmmaking* at `http://learnaboutfilm.com/making-a-film/equipment-for-low-budget-filmmaking/`.

3. **Accept that audio enhances your video**: Next to lighting, audio is often the most important element of a professional video, yet it is frequently overlooked. We often see with our ears: high-quality audio can improve low-quality video; likewise, low-quality audio can make high-quality video seem amateur. Fortunately, recording professional audio doesn't have to be difficult; the most important element is using a microphone specifically for the presenter. Avoid using the camera's internal microphone as your only source of audio as it captures all of the noises and echoes in the room where you are recording. If your camera does not have an external audio input, that's okay. Zoom and Tascam sell external audio recorders to which you can connect a separate microphone. Also, make sure there are no outside noises such as street traffic, HVAC hums, or extraneous talking when you are recording.

To learn more about recording high-quality audio for your videos, watch *Filmmaking 101 - How to Record High Quality Audio on a Budget* at `https://youtu.be/k0rHak6aJl8` or read the article *Recording Audio for Business Videos* from Wistia at `http://wistia.com/library/recording-audio-for-business-video`.

4. **Focus your audience's attention with lighting**: Shadows and blown-out shots are your enemy. Shadows happen when there is insufficient lighting and/or objects in between the lighting source and the subject being recorded. A blown out image occurs when there is too much bright light entering the lens and the camera picks up nothing but blindingly white space. Ensure that there are no bright lights or windows behind you and that you stay away from harsh overhead light. You also want to have three points of lighting: one light will be your main light source, known as the **key light,** that faces your subject. Another light, facing your subject from the opposite angle that fills in soft shadows is your **fill light**. The final lighting source is called the **back light**; typically above and behind your subject, it provides a depth of field that creates a professional appearance in your video. For reference have a look at the screen capture image given next from Steven DiCasa's YouTube video *Filmmaking 101 - Three Point Lighting Tutorial* in which a typical three-point lighting configuration is shown:

 Learn to light your video professionally, even if you have a modest budget, as shown in the YouTube video *Filmmaking 101 - Three Point Lighting Tutorial* at https://youtu.be/j_Sov3xmgwg or read the Wistia article *Lighting on the Fly* at http://wistia.com/library/lighting-on-the-fly for more knowledge.

5. **Upgrade your video's aesthetics with small accessories**: Never underestimate the big impact small items can have on your videos. With some exceptions, a tripod is a necessity for studio video recording; you can find tripods in a variety of shapes and sizes for a reasonable price at almost any electronics retailer. You can even get a miniature tripod for your smartphone, but selfie sticks are optional! If you aren't in a position to afford the professional-grade studio lighting that we discussed in the previous section, then portable clamp lights provide a flexible and professional alternative for minimal cost and effort. In addition to the lamps, you will need compact fluorescent lights (CFL), which are also easy to find at Home Depot or similar stores. Just be sure to buy the daylight bulbs with a color temperature of at least 5000K (5,000 degrees Kelvin). The following picture is a CFL display in Home Depot:

 Learn how to shoot video with an iPhone in the Wistia article *Shooting Video with an iPhone* at `http://wistia.com/library/shooting-video-with-an-iphone`.

6. **Frame your shots thoughtfully**: Using the rule of thirds you can frame your shot to create a professional look for your videos. Imagine a grid over your field of view that divides the frame into nine sections. This creates reference points that act as guides for framing the image. Your goal is to have the subject appear in either the lower-third or upper-third sections; either top to bottom or left to right. You want to avoid having your subject appear right in the middle of the frame; the face of your subject should appear in the top third of the frame, and their body should fill the bottom two-thirds of the screen. However, the rule of thirds might not apply with a picture-in-picture style, where the instructor will only have his face shown on top of a slide. The following screenshot from the Vimeo video school lesson *Framing and Composition* demonstrates the rule of thirds:

 Increase your understanding of video framing and composition in the Vimeo video school lesson *Framing and Composition* at https://vimeo.com/videoschool/lesson/8/framing-and-composition.

7. **Edit professionally and economically**: Editing your educational videos doesn't have to be a time-consuming process; there are free or inexpensive video editing programs that allow you to add in basic graphics that can enhance your video's production quality without requiring a lot of training. The key is to not use products that have more bells and whistles than you need. For many, professional-level editing software is too robust for their needs and will only make the process more complicated. Consider basic iMovie or Premiere Elements software to lay out your video footage, eliminate any unnecessary elements, and add in basic text graphics.

Improve your videos with the help of editing lessons from the Vimeo video school at `https://vimeo.com/videoschool/archive/editing` and learn to anticipate the editing process while recording in the Wistia article *Shooting for the Edit* at `http://wistia.com/library/shooting-for-the-edit`.

If this is your first time creating videos for an online course, you should anticipate a learning curve. Even if your university has a video production department, you will still need to understand and adapt to the production process. Nevertheless, you will improve over time, but the important thing is to simply get started.

Connect with Dominique on LinkedIn at `https://www.linkedin.com/in/dominiquesamario` or on Twitter at `https://twitter.com/domsamario`.

Video post-production processes

Once you've recorded your videos, you need to edit them and then generate the video files. Both Mac and Windows operating systems come with native programs: iMovie for Mac and Windows Movie Maker for Windows. While these programs might be suitable for basic video production, you might find them limited and too underpowered.

Consider the following list of licensed and open source software solutions; while it is by no means exhaustive, it should give you a strong start:

Licensed Video Editors	Links
Adobe Premiere Elements	`http://www.adobe.com/products/premiere-elements.html`
Adobe Premiere Pro Creative Cloud	`http://www.adobe.com/mena_en/products/premiere.html`
Apple Final Cut Pro	`https://www.apple.com/final-cut-pro/`
Corel Video Studio Pro	`http://www.videostudiopro.com/en/products/videostudio/pro/`
Corel Video Studio Ultimate	`http://www.videostudiopro.com/en/products/videostudio/ultimate/`
Pinnacle Studio	`http://www.pinnaclesys.com/PublicSite/us/Products/studio/`
Sony Vegas	`http://www.sonycreativesoftware.com/vegassoftware`

Licensed Video Editors	Links
TechSmith Camtasia Studio	`https://www.techsmith.com/camtasia.html`
TechSmith Jing	`https://www.techsmith.com/jing.htmlhttp://www.techsmith.com/jing.html`
TechSmith Snagit	`https://www.techsmith.com/snagit.htmlhttp://www.techsmith.com/snagit.html`

Open Source Video Editors	Links
Avidemux	`http://fixounet.free.fr/avidemux/`
Blender	`http://www.blender.org/`
Cinelerra	`http://cinelerra-cv.org/`
KDEnlive	`https://kdenlive.org/`
Lightworks	`http://www.lwks.com/`
OpenShot	`http://www.openshot.org/`
Pitvi	`http://www.pitivi.org/`

Reducing the video file size

One issue you might encounter while editing your videos is that the source files (that is, the raw files containing the unedited content you recorded) are very large in size; some might also be several gigabytes. To make the files more manageable for editing, you should explore options to either compress the videos or to convert them to a file type that is smaller.

Some of the video editing software options previously mentioned in this chapter might contain a video compression function, but there are also some third-party options you can use before you import the file into your video editor.

One option is a program called Video to Video, which is available for free download. In the following example, an MP4 file that was 669.93 MB in size was converted to a smaller type of MP4 file, which reduced it to 45.52 MB. This made it much easier to work with!

 Download Video to Video at `http://www.videotovideo.org/download/` or consider another program, Handbrake, which you can find at `https://handbrake.fr/downloads.php`.

If you find yourself needing to reduce the size of your video files, take some time to review the following resources for a possible solution:

- About.com: *33 Free Video Converter Programs and Online Services* available at `http://pcsupport.about.com/od/fileextensions/tp/free-video-converter.htm`

- How-To Geek: *Use Handbrake to Compress Large Video Files to Play on Your Tablet or Phone* available at `http://www.howtogeek.com/199637/use-handbrake-to-compress-large-video-files-to-play-on-your-tablet-or-phone/`

- Learning Solutions Magazine: *Video Compression Secrets: Smaller Files, Better Quality* available at `http://www.learningsolutionsmag.com/articles/1203/video-compression-secrets-smaller-files-better-quality`

- Reducing Video: *When Size Does Matter* available at `http://www.freemake.com/blog/reducing-video-when-size-does-matter/`

- Screencast Video Services: *Shrink Down Those Giant Video Files* available at `http://www.vademogirl.com/when-you-get-complaints-that-its-just-too-big/`

- Video Grabber: *How to reduce video size* available at `http://www.videograbber.net/reduce-video-size.html`

- wikiHow: *How to Compress Video* available at `http://www.wikihow.com/Compress-Video`

edX video specifications

The last step in editing videos is publishing the file for use. Video editors present you with many different options, so it is important to know which specifications to use for your edX videos.

The edX video player supports the .mp4, .ogg, and .mpeg formats. However, to ensure that standard browsers can play your video, edX recommends you produce your video in the .mp4 or .webm format. If you publish your videos to YouTube, you can also make them available for download as one of the additional supported file types.

 WebM is an open media file format designed for use on the Web. WebM files include video streams compressed with the VP8 or VP9 video codec, audio streams compressed with the Vorbis or Opus audio codecs, and WebVTT text tracks. The WebM file structure is based on the Matroska media container. For more information on WebM, see http://www.webmproject.org/.

While creating your video files, note that edX recommends the following compression specs:

Output	Edited Files	Publish to YouTube	Publish as an Amazon S3 Downloadable File
Codec	H.264 .mp4	H.264 "main concept" .mp4	H.264 "x264" .mp4
Resolution and Frame Rate	1920 x 1080, progressive, 29.97 fps	1920 x 1080, progressive, 29.97 fps	1280 x 720, progressive, 29.97 fps
Aspect	1.0	1.0	1.0
Bit Rate	VBR, 2 pass	VBR, 2 pass	VBR, 2 pass
Target VBR	32 mbps	5 mbps	1 mbps
Max VBR	40 mbps	7.5 mbps	1.5 mbps
Audio	Linear AAC 48kHz / 256 kbps	AAC 44.1 / 192 kbps	AAC 44.1 / 192 kbps

Transcripts for your videos

A useful feature of edX is its ability to display a synchronized transcript as your video plays. This helps students follow along with what you're saying, especially if you are explaining complex concepts and/or if a student's first language is not English.

One unique benefit of including a transcript is that it scrolls automatically while the video plays within the edX platform; if a student clicks on a word within the transcript, the video will rewind or fast-forward to that word (or phrase) in the video. Instructors can also allow students to download the transcript in different formats including a `.pdf` or `.srt` file for reading offline.

Have a look at an example of the transcript from *edX101 How to Create an edX Course* :

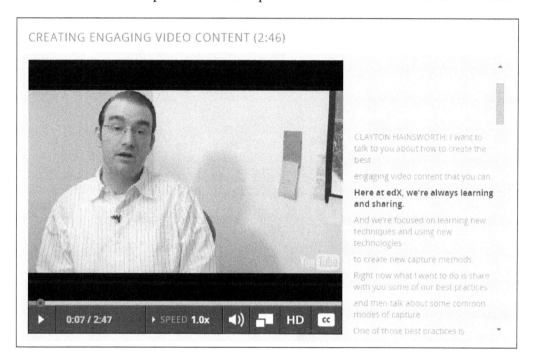

For the transcript to automatically play in sync with your course video, it must be a .srt file. EdX will detect whether or not a YouTube video you've added to a course includes a transcript or not, as illustrated in the following screenshots. In the first one, edX has detected a suitable transcript that you can then download, edit, and replace if you desire, as shown here:

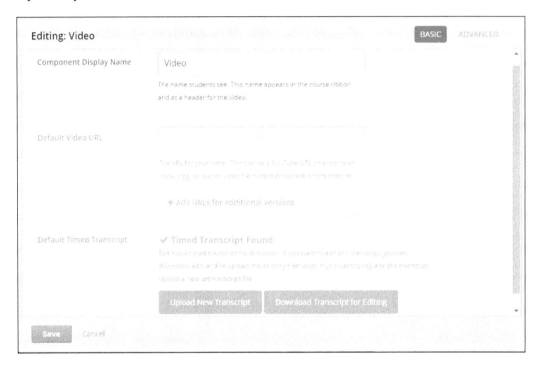

In the next example, edX cannot find a usable transcript, so one will need to be created:

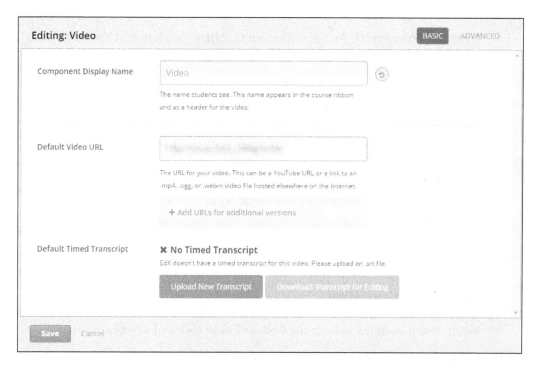

You can create the transcript yourself or work with a third-party vendor that provides captioning services to create the .srt file. EdX works with Cambridge, Massachusetts-based 3Play Media.

 Visit the website of 3Play Media to learn more about their video captioning, transcription, and subtitle services at http://www.3playmedia.com/.

YouTube will automatically generate a transcript for each of your uploaded videos, but their accuracy is often questionable. You can edit .srt files using any of the following options:

- **Notepad (Windows)**: As `.srt` files are text files, you can edit them with relative ease using the standard Windows Notepad application. Note: exercise caution here. The transcript files have a rigid format that must be followed or some subtitles may not appear to the student. It is better to use a computer-assisted editor.

- **Subtitle Edit** (`http://www.nikse.dk/subtitleedit/`): Subtitle Edit is an open source editor for video subtitles; with Subtitle Edit you can easily adjust a subtitle if it is out of sync with the video.

- **Subtitle Workshop** (`http://www.urusoft.net/products.php?cat=sw`): Subtitle Workshop is a freeware subtitle editing tool that supports all the subtitle formats.

- **SRT Subtitles Editor** (`http://download.cnet.com/SRTEd-SRT-Subtitles-Editor/3000-13631_4-75884617.html`): SRT Subtitles Editor is a graphical editor for SRT subtitles and closed captions.

- **YouTube captions editor** (`https://support.google.com/youtube/answer/2734705`): The YouTube captions editor allows you to quickly and easily make changes to both the text and time codes of your captions.

Additional instructions about how to create alternate transcripts and add them to your course will be discussed in *Chapter 5*, *Integrating the Curriculum*.

YouTube best practices

An additional component of producing videos is managing them once they're uploaded to YouTube. Once you've uploaded more than around two dozen videos, you will need to click through several pages of your video manager to find your videos.

This can prove challenging if you teach many courses, each with its own series of videos. To remedy this, be sure to create playlists for each course and add each video you recorded for that class to its playlist. This will let you organize your videos; moreover, you can also share the playlist for a course with your students.

Take a look at the following example of a video being added to a playlist:

Here is a screen shot of a series of videos in a playlist:

Keep in mind that the edX video player defaults to, and is optimized for, YouTube videos. However, it is equally important to remember that YouTube might not be available in all countries.

Usually these restrictions can be circumvented by accessing the Internet through a virtual private network (VPN). A VPN creates a secure and private connection within a public Internet connection or a private network, freeing a user from restrictions imposed by those networks and shielding their activity from "prying eyes".

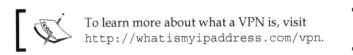

To learn more about what a VPN is, visit
`http://whatismyipaddress.com/vpn`.

However, a VPN isn't always a realistic option for everyone. Given that reality, edX encourages you to upload a copy of your video on a third-party site such as Amazon S3 or a web server of your own (or one your university or company manages). That way, when a student views a video in your course and the YouTube video won't play, the backup video will either begin playing automatically or can be downloaded.

Summary

In this chapter, we explored the idea and intent of instructional videos, learned several key video production pointers, reviewed post-production processes, explained the process for creating transcripts for your videos, and outlined how to create playlists on YouTube for each of your courses.

In *Chapter 5, Integrating the Curriculum*, we will revisit some of these tasks while reviewing related concepts as we further explore adding curriculum you've created to your edX course.

But prior to that, in *Chapter 4, Designing Exercises*, we will investigate how to create additional elements of curriculum for your edX course. Specifically, we define problem components, review common problems, create advanced problems, devise specialized problems, and understand open responses.

4
Designing Exercises

In her 1981 hit single "Physical", Olivia Newton John sings about the benefits of exercise, telling us "Let's get physical… Let me hear your body talk". While the song certainly had additional interpretations, it did reveal some scientific truth.

It's an anecdotally accepted idea that physical exercise has a positive impact on your brain. Now two Stanford University researchers have proven it. In their April 2014 *Journal of Experimental Psychology: Learning, Memory, and Cognition* article *Give Your Ideas Some Legs: The Positive Effect of Walking on Creative Thinking*, authors Marily Oppezzo, MS, RD, PhD and Daniel Schwartz, MA, PhD made the following discovery:

> *"Walking boosts creative ideation in real time and shortly after... Walking opens up the free flow of ideas, and it is a simple and robust solution to the goals of increasing creativity and increasing physical activity"*.

Their research involved 176 participants completing four experiments designed to gauge creative thinking. Oppezzo and Schwartz discovered that a walk as short as eight minutes increased creativity by an average of 60% over those participants who remained seated.

Likewise, exercises in your course let your students "stretch their intellectual legs". They also give them an opportunity to engage in generative learning by letting them make connections between their existing knowledge and new information acquired in your class. Exercises are an effective way to help your students learn while making their learning experience more enjoyable overall.

After reading this chapter, you should know how to:

- See the student view of problem components
- View the Studio view of problem components
- Edit problem components

- Create problems with edX's editors
- Understand available exercises and tools
- Understand content experiments.

The student view of problem components

You can use Studio to create an array of exercises for your course; there are even templates for the more common ones. Depending on your course's learning objectives, you will choose from the following four types of exercises:

- General exercises and tools
- Image-based exercises and tools
- Multiple-choice exercises and tools
- STEM exercises and tools

At the core of every edX exercise, there is a problem component; it is the way you add tools and interactive exercises or tools that are automatically graded in your class curriculum. During this process, you will use one of the following three types of components:

- HTML
- Problem
- Advanced

All problems have several component parts including the elements described and pictured in the following screenshot from *UTAustinX: UT.7.01x Foundations of Data Analysis*:

 View the "About" page for this course at `https://www.edx.org/ course/utaustinx/utaustinx-ut-7-01x-foundations- data-2641#.VGfGBPmUdIw`.

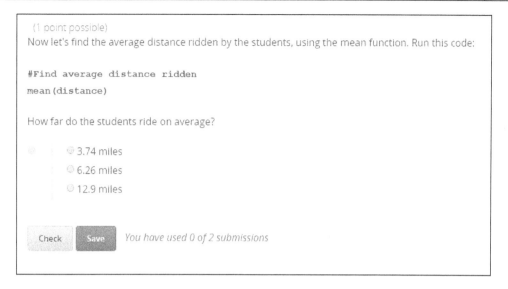

- **Attempts**: Choose a specific number of attempts or allow unlimited attempts.
- **Check button**: Clicking **Check** reveals if the answer is correct or not. If it is correct, a green check mark appears. If not, a red **X** is displayed. Studio will also save the grade and current status of the problem.
- **Correct answer**: Most problems require you to specify a correct answer that edX will then grade. The following screenshot shows an incorrect answer displayed to a student:

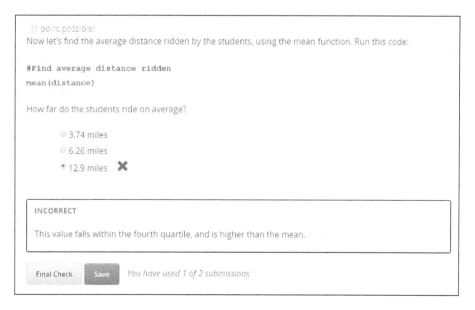

Conversely, this is how a correct answer looks to a student:

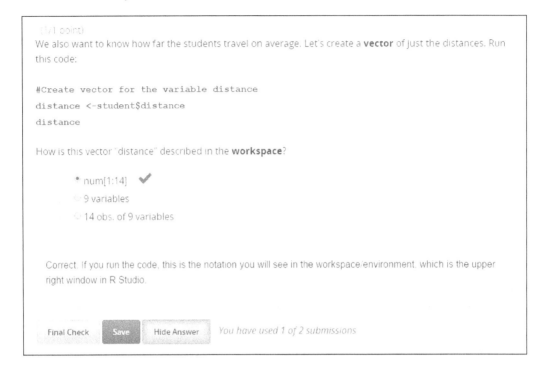

- **Due date**: This is the date when the answer to a problem must be submitted. A past due problem is considered closed and won't have a **Check** button; answers will not be accepted and feedback will not be provided for this.

> Students can view questions, solutions, and revealed explanations for past due problems, but they are unable to check their submission, submit new responses, or change an earlier score. Some problem attributes are not immediately visible; you can control them in Studio.

- **Explanation**: You may include an explanation that appears when a student clicks the gray **Show Answer** button.

- **Feedback**: When a student clicks the gray **Check** button, a green check or a red **X** shows.

- **Grading**: The instructor may specify whether a group of problems is graded or not. If a group of problems is graded, a clock icon appears for that assignment in the course accordion.

- **Hide Answer button**: Clicking the gray **Hide Answer** button conceals the shown answer. An example of the **Hide Answer** button is shown here:

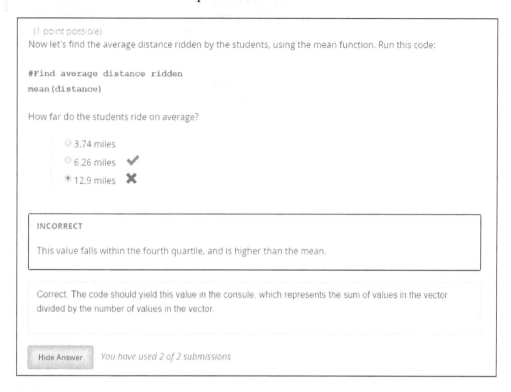

- **Label**: This provides improved accessibility for students with disabilities; it should be descriptive and contain part or all of the text of the question in the problem. Most templates provide space for a label.
- **Problem text**: This is the text of the problem; it may contain HTML formatting.
- **Randomization**: You can specify whether a problem uses randomly generated numbers that vary among students.
- **Reset button**: This clears the student input, so the problem looks the way it did before an answer was attempted.
- **Response field**: Students enter answers in the response fields; the look of the field will differ based on the problem type.
- **Rendered answer**: For some types of problems, edX uses MathJax to render plain text as beautiful math.

"Beautiful Math" is the result of text a student enters for a problem being converted to a symbolic expression, which will then appear below that field. Math expression problems can include unknown variables and much more complex symbolic expressions, unlike numerical input problems that only allow integers and a few select constants.

- **Save button**: Clicking the blue **Save** button records a student's response without submitting it for grading; this lets a student stop working and return to the problem later. Have a look at the **Save** button function in the following screenshot:

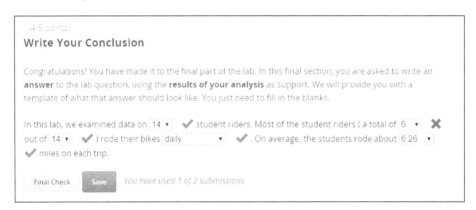

- **Show Answer**: Selecting the gray **Show Answer** button reveals the correct answer and an accompanying explanation. This is optional; you determine whether the **Show Answer** button is visible to students or not. See the **Show Answer** functionality here:

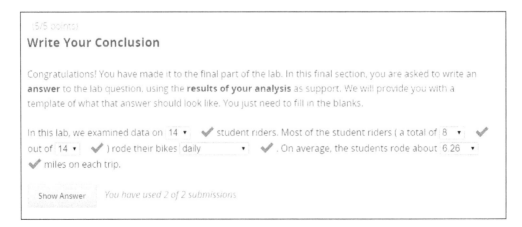

- **Weight**: Different problems can be given different values.

The Studio view of problem components

Now that you've seen the student view of problem components, let's take a peek at the Studio view. We will review the process of creating problems in *Chapter 5, Integrating the Curriculum*, but it's helpful to understand your options before you dive into them.

If you don't yet have access to edX, you can explore Studio by accessing the free edX sandbox as shown here:

1. Go to `https://studio.sandbox.edx.org/`.
2. Click the gray **Sign In** button in the upper right-hand corner:

3. Enter an **Email Address:** `staff@example.com`.
4. Enter a **Password:** of `edx`.
5. Click the blue **SIGN IN TO EDX STUDIO** button.

6. Scroll through the list of available courses, selecting the **edX Demonstration Course** title or the blue **View Live** button to enter the course.

 This allows you to simultaneously view the **edX Demonstration Course** in the Sandbox and manage the course in Studio in the Sandbox. Keep in mind that the Sandbox is typically cleared and reset on a weekly basis, so don't expect changes you make to courses, or courses you add there, to remain functional for an extended period of time.

7. Select the exercise you would like to review in the Sandbox Studio; let's look at the **Week 1** Section | the **Homework – Question Styles** Subsection | the **Mathematical Expressions** unit:

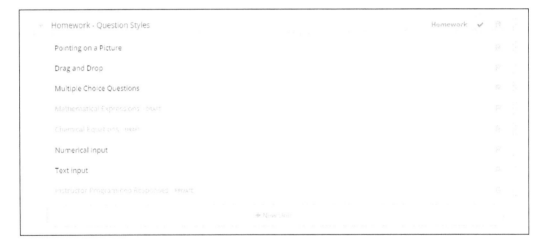

From here you can click through the buttons to view the backend of a problem or, if desired, make changes to the course itself. Let's explore how to do that in the next section.

Editing problem components

Once you've accessed a problem component, you can edit it as needed. Within the Sandbox you can edit freely but, if you're in a live course, be careful for the following three reasons:

1. Once a student submits their answer, edX stores their response, their score, and the maximum score possible. For problems that have a Maximum Attempts setting greater than 1, edX updates these values for each new response.

2. If you change a problem or its attributes, all of the information already entered for that problem is not updated, potentially giving that student an incorrect answer or no score at all.

3. If you leave the problem unchanged but instead modify its weight, the student's score will be updated when their **Progress** page refreshes. In a live section, students will see the effect of these changes.

However, if you need to change a problem in a published course, you have the following two options:

1. Increase the number of attempts for the problem and then ask your students to resubmit their answer; this allows them to work around the previous limit.

2. Delete the prior problem component and create a new one using the updated content and settings; then ask your students to resubmit their answer. If the edits you make are minor, you can duplicate the problem component.

 When such a change is needed, as a courtesy to your students you should send them an email message informing them of the change and letting them know what action(s) to take in response. For more information about sending email to students, refer to the *Messages to Students* section of *Chapter 7, Facilitating Your Course*.

Taking note of the issues and options explained above, let's review how to edit a problem component, starting from where we last left off at the **Week 1** section | the **Homework – Question Styles** subsection | the **Mathematical Expressions** unit:

1. Click **edit a draft** to revise an exercise that was previously published.

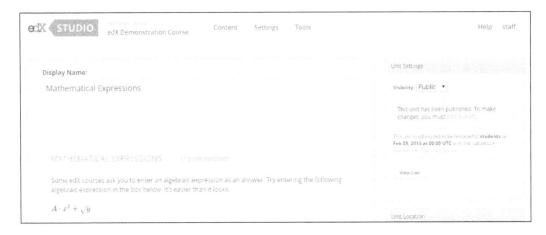

2. Click on the **EDIT** icon in the problem to open either **Simple Editor** or **Advanced Editor**.

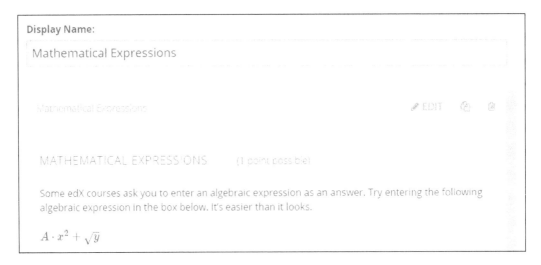

3. Make any necessary changes to the exercise using the available editor and click the blue **Save** button when it's finished.

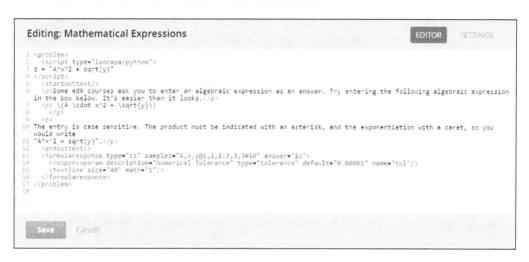

4. Make any necessary changes to the settings using the available editor—**Simple Editor** or **Advanced Editor**—and click the blue **Save** button when finished.

5. See the next section, *Creating problems with edX's Editors*, for additional information about **Simple Editor** and **Advanced Editor**.

6. Select **replace it with this draft** to implement your changes. You can also click the blue **Delete Draft** button to discard your edits.

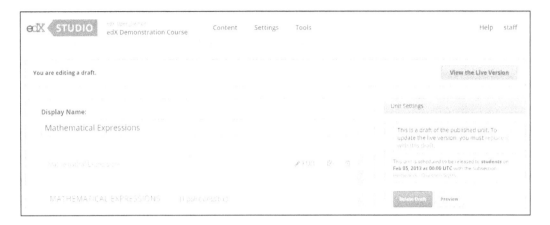

Creating problems with edX's editors

Now that you're familiar with Studio, what problems you create in it and how they will look to your students, let's review how to create a problem using the two available editor tools: Simple Editor and Advanced Editor.

With the **Simple Editor** you can edit problems without needing to know XML, the backbone of edX's functionality. There are templates for common problem types such as multiple-choice and text input along with a user-friendly toolbar that you can use to format text in your problem.

Offering more functionality, the **Advanced Editor** converts your problem to XML, which you can then edit. Also, much like the **Simple Editor**, the **Advanced Editor** provides several problem templates. But, it is important to know that, once you switch to the **Advanced Editor**, you cannot revert to the **Simple Editor**.

Now let's walk through the steps you will take to create a new problem:

1. Determine the section and subsection where you will add your problem or click the gray **+ New Subsection** button to create a new subsection (it turns blue when you hover your mouse over it).

 For this exercise, a subsection titled *EdX E-Learning Course Development* was added to example *Week 1: Getting Started in the Sandbox Studio* of the *edX Demonstration Course*.

2. Click the gray **+ New Unit** button to create a new unit in the subsection you selected or created (it turns blue after you have opened the subsection).

 For this exercise, a unit titled *EdX E-Learning Course Development* was added to example *Week 1: Getting Started in the Sandbox Studio* of the *edX Demonstration Course*.

3. Name your unit *EdX E-Learning Course Development Problem, as* in the following example, and click the green **Problem** button.

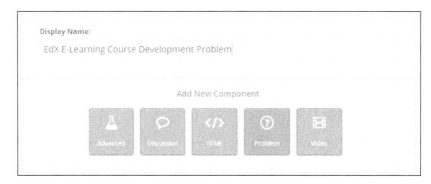

4. Consider the **Common Problem Types**; some options include:
   - **Checkbox**: Students choose from a list of possible answers
   - **Dropdown**: Students select their answer from a drop-down list
   - **Multiple Choice**: Students select one answer from a list of several choices presented directly below the question
   - **Numerical Input**: Students input answers that include only integers, fractions, and a few common constants and operators
   - **Text Input**: Students type a short text answer to a question

   The following screenshot displays the list of available **Common Problem Types** noted in the preceding bullet points:

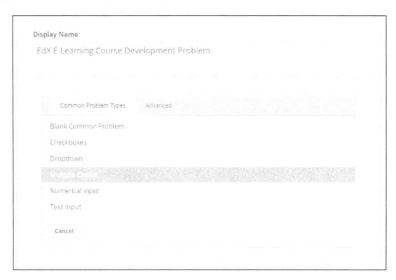

5. Consider using **Advanced** problems; some options include:

   ° **Circuit Schematic Builder**: Students create and modify circuits using an interactive grid and submit computer-generated analyses of the circuits for grading.

   ° **Custom JavaScript**: Incorporate problem types that you've created in HTML into Studio using an IFrame.

   ° **Drag and Drop**: Students drag text or objects to a specific location on an image.

   ° **Image Mapped Input**: Students click a specific location on an image to identify a correct answer.

   ° **Math Expression Input**: Students enter a mathematical expression as text such as $e=m*c\wedge2$.

   ° **Problem with Adaptive Hint**: Based on the responses students enter, these problems can provide feedback or hints; text input or multiple-choice problems can contain adaptive hints.

   ° **Problem Written in LaTeX**: Use this to convert problems into the edX format that you've already written in LaTeX. This problem type is a prototype and might not be fully supported.

   ° **Write-Your-Own-Grader**: Evaluate students' responses using an embedded Python script that you create; these problems can be of any type.

The following screenshot displays the list of available **Advanced** problems noted in the preceding bullet points:

6. Click **Edit** in the upper right-hand corner of the problem to open the **Simple Editor**. For this example, we chose the **Multiple Choice** option from the **Common Problem Types** list.

 You can also click the double paper icon to the right of **Edit** to duplicate the problem in the same subsection or click the trashcan icon to delete the problem.

7. Review the problem in the **Simple Editor**, make your changes, and then click the blue **Save** button. You can also click **Cancel** to return to the problem.

8. Open a list of formatting hints using the toolbar. Additionally, you can create any one of the following problem types:
    - ◦ A level 1 heading
    - ◦ An explanation that displays when students click **Show Answer**
    - ◦ Checkbox options
    - ◦ Drop-down options
    - ◦ Multiple choice options
    - ◦ Numerical input options
    - ◦ Text input options

The following screenshot shows the **Advanced Editor** for a multiple choice problem:

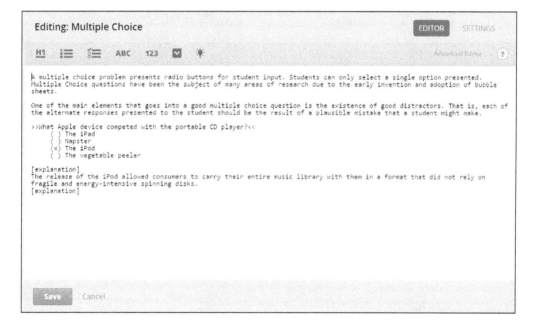

9. Select **Advanced Editor** to switch from the **Simple Editor** and have direct access to the XML functionality.

 Reminder: You can't revert to the **Simple Editor** once you've switched to the **Advanced Editor**. A pop-up window warns you of this and asks you to click a gray **OK** button to continue or a gray **Cancel** button to discontinue the change.

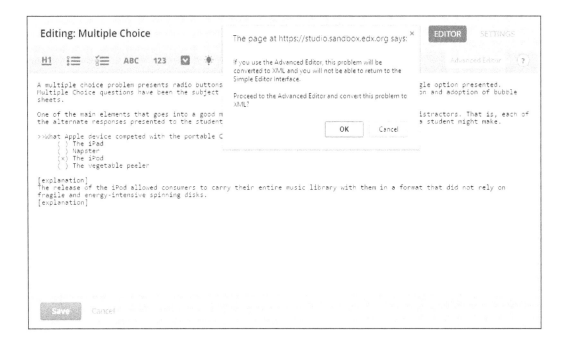

10. Use the **Advanced Editor** to make your desired changes in XML:

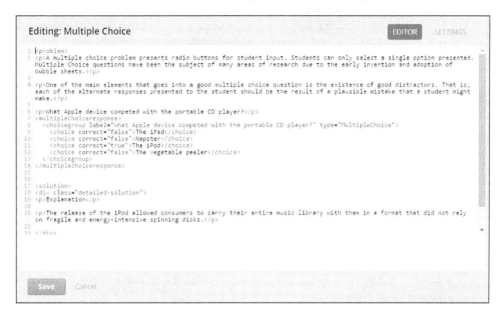

11. Edit the problem settings by clicking the gray **Settings** button and then the blue **Save** button when finished. The available functions in this include:

   ° **Display Name**: This is the name of your problem; it appears as a heading over the problem and in the course ribbon across the top of the page.

   ° **Maximum Attempts**: This is the number of times a student can attempt to answer a problem. The **Maximum Attempts** advanced setting default is set to "unlimited". If this is changed, the **Maximum Attempts** setting for individual problems defaults to that number and cannot be set to unlimited.

   ° **Problem Weight**: This is the maximum number of points possible for the problem; the problem weight appears next to the problem title.

   ° **Computing Score**: This is the score that is the result of the following formula: *Weight × (Correct Answers / Response Fields) = Score*. In this equation, "Score" is the numerical points that the student receives, "Weight" is the problem's maximum number possible, "Correct Answers" is the number of response fields with correct answers, and "Response Fields" is the total number of fields available.

   ° **Randomization**: This specifies whether or not certain values change each time a different student accesses the problem or each time a single student tries to answer the problem.

Specifying this **Randomization** setting is different from problem randomization; the **Randomization** setting randomizes variables in a single problem while problem randomization presents different problems or versions of the same problem to different students.

- ○ **Show Answer**: This specifies whether the problem shows the answer to the student after an answer is submitted.
- ○ **Reset**: Students can click **Reset** to clear anything they've entered but have not yet submitted; they can then submit a different answer.

 If the student has submitted an answer, clicking **Reset** clears the submission. If the problem contains randomized variables and randomization is set to **On**, then clicking **Reset** changes the values the student sees. If the **Maximum** was reached, the **Reset** button will no longer be visible.

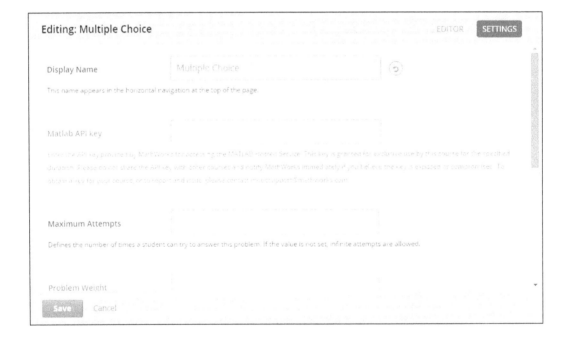

 You can also click **Cancel** to return to the problem template.

12. Click the gray **View Live** button in the **Unit Settings** section to switch out of Studio into the live version of the course you're working on, as shown in the following screenshot:

13. Navigate to the location of the problem you were working on to preview how it appears to staff and students. Take a look at the following screenshot for this:

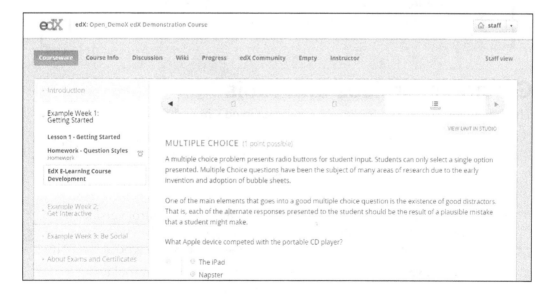

Exercises and tools

You can create a great number of exercises and tools for your course using Studio; there are templates already available in Studio for many of them. Course teams will also create exercises that don't yet have templates in Studio, so in many cases you won't be starting from zero.

Depending on the exercise or tool you need to create, you will use an HTML, problem, or advanced component. Definitions for each are presented here, organized into one of the following four possible types:

- General exercises and tools

- Image-based exercises and tools

- Multiple-choice exercises and tools

- STEM exercises and tools

For details beyond the overview for each, you are directed to visit section **6.1 Creating Exercises and Tools**, of the online documentation for edX, **Building and Running an edX Course**. There you will find pages for each exercise or tool listed below with an example of each along with all the files, code, and step-by-step instructions you need.

 You can find section **6.1 Creating Exercises and Tools**, of **Building and Running an edX Course** at `http://edx.readthedocs.org/projects/edx-partner-course-staff/en/latest/exercises_tools/create_exercises_and_tools.html`.

General exercises and tools

The general exercises and tools you can create in edX include:

- **Annotation Problem**: Ask students to respond to questions about a specific block of text; it appears above the text when the student hovers their mouse over the highlighted text, so students can think about the question as they read.

- **Conditional Module**: Create a conditional module to control versions of content that groups of students see. For example, students who answer **Yes** to a poll question will see a different block of text from those who answer **No**.

- **Custom JavaScript Problem**: Create a custom problem or tool using JavaScript and then add the problem or tool directly into Studio.

- **External Grader**: An external grader receives responses to a problem, processes them, and returns feedback with a grade to the course; this is useful in software programming courses where students submit complex code.

- **Google Instant Hangout Tool**: Students can participate in hangouts for your course, interact via live video and voice, share screens, watch videos together, and collaborate on documents. You will need to share the Google+ hangout link with your students so that they can participate.

- **IFrame Tool**: Integrate ungraded exercises and tools from any Internet site into an HTML component within your course.

- **LTI Component**: Add an external learning application or a non-PDF textbook to edX Studio.

- **Open Response Assessment Problems**: Students receive feedback on written responses of varying lengths as well as files such as computer code or images that the students upload. Open response assessments include self-assessment and peer assessment.

- **Poll Tool**: This tool helps you run polls in your course so that your students can share opinions about different questions.

- **Problem with Adaptive Hint**: This evaluates a student's response and then gives the student feedback or a hint based on that response, so the student is more likely to answer correctly on the next attempt. These problems can be text input or multiple-choice types.

- **Problem Written in LaTeX**: Use this problem type to easily convert the code for problems written in LaTeX into XML.

- **Text Input Problem**: Students enter text into a response field that can include numbers, letters, and special characters such as punctuation marks.

- **Word Cloud Tool**: This arranges text entered by students into a colorful visual graphic viewable by students.

- **Write-Your-Own-Grader Problem**: The grader uses a custom Python script embedded in the problem to evaluate a student's response or provide hints; this works with any type of problem.

 Find all of the files, code, and step-by-step instructions you need to create general exercises and tools in **Building and Running an edX Course** at http://edx.readthedocs.org/projects/edx-partner-course-staff/en/latest/exercises_tools/create_exercises_and_tools.html#general-exercises-and-tools.

Image-based exercises and tools

The image-based exercises and tools that you can create in edX include:

- **Drag and Drop Problem**: Students respond to a question by dragging text or objects to a specific location within an image; this is useful for problems that ask a student to identify various elements of an image

- **Full Screen Image Tool**: Students can enlarge an image to fill the whole browser window; this is especially useful when an image has a great amount of detail

- **Image Mapped Input Problem**: Students click inside a defined area within an image by including coordinates in the body of the problem

- **Zooming Image Tool**: This enlarges sections of an image so that students can see that particular section in detail

Find all of the files, code, and step-by-step instructions you need to create image-based exercises and tools in **Building and Running an edX Course** at http://edx.readthedocs.org/projects/ edx-partner-course-staff/en/latest/exercises_tools/ create_exercises_and_tools.html#image-based- exercises-and-tools.

Multiple-choice exercises and tools

Multiple-choice exercises and tools that you can create in edX include:

- **Checkbox Problem**: Here, students select one or more options from a list of possible answers that are visible directly below a question

- **Dropdown Problem**: Here, students choose an answer from a list of options in a drop-down list that displays after a student clicks the drop-down arrow

- **Multiple Choice Problem**: Here, students select one option from a list of answer options visible directly below a question

- **Multiple Choice and Numerical Input Problem**: This combines a multiple-choice problem and a numerical input problem where students choose one response from several options

Find all of the files, code, and step-by-step instructions you need to create multiple-choice exercises and tools in **Building and Running an edX Course** at `http://edx.readthedocs.org/projects/ edx-partner-course-staff/en/latest/exercises_tools/ create_exercises_and_tools.html#multiple-choice- exercises-and-tools.`

STEM exercises and tools

STEM exercises and tools that you can create in edX include:

- **Chemical Equation Problem**: In this case, students enter text representing a chemical equation; the grader evaluates the submission by using a Python script you create and embed within the problem.

- **Circuit Schematic Builder Problem**: Here, students arrange circuit elements on an interactive grid and submit a DC, AC, or transient analysis of their circuit for grading.

- **Gene Explorer Tool**: This simulates the transcription, splicing, processing, and translation of a small hypothetical eukaryotic gene. After students make specific mutations in a gene sequence, the tool calculates and displays the effects of the mutations on the mRNA and protein.

- **Math Expression Input**: Here students enter mathematical expressions to answer a question. These problems can include unknown variables and more complex symbolic expressions (such as $E = mc^2$). You can also specify a correct answer explicitly or with a Python script.

- **Molecule Editor Tool**: Students draw molecules that follow the rules for covalent bond formation and formal charge, even if the molecules are chemically impossible or unstable, or they do not exist in living systems.

- **Numerical Input**: Here, students enter numbers or specific and relatively simple mathematical expressions to answer a question. These problems accept integers and numbers written in decimal notation (for example, `3.14159`); as an instructor, you will need to specify a tolerance limit in the accepted answers (as an interval) to account for rounding errors. You can specify a margin of error and a correct answer explicitly or with a Python script.

- **Periodic Table Tool**: This is an interactive periodic table of the elements showing detailed information as the student moves the mouse over each element.

- **Protex Protein Builder Tool**: Here, students create specified protein shapes by stringing together amino acids.

 Find all of the files, code, and step-by-step instructions you need to create STEM exercises and tools in **Building and Running an edX Course** at `http://edx.readthedocs.org/projects/edx-partner-course-staff/en/latest/exercises_tools/create_exercises_and_tools.html#stem-exercises-and-tools`.

Content experiments

Consider creating A/B split tests to show different content to groups of students. You can then compare the performance of the students in each group, gaining added insight into the effectiveness of your curriculum.

 To learn more about A/B split testing, have a look at the Wikipedia article at `http://en.wikipedia.org/wiki/A/B_testing`.

You can have multiple content experiments active simultaneously in your course; each experiment can use the same groups, or you can have each content experiment operate independently.

 If two experiments share the same grouping, any student in Group A for the first experiment will also be in Group A for the second one. If you want your content experiments to operate independently, you must assign different groupings to each content experiment so that students are randomly assigned to each.

Enabling content experiments requires you to add `"split_test"` (the internal edX name for a content experiment) to the **Advanced Modules List** in **Advanced Settings**, as shown in the following steps:

1. Select **Advanced Settings** from the **Settings** menu at the top of the screen:

2. Locate **Advanced Modules List** on the **Advanced Settings** page.

3. Add `"split_test"` in the **Advanced Modules List** field, making sure you include the double quotation marks.

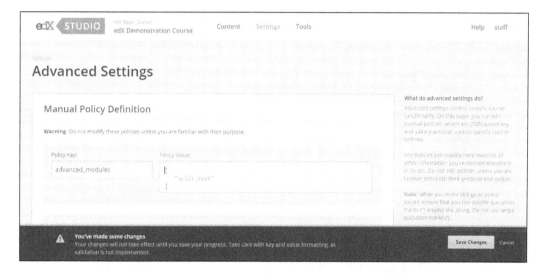

4. At the bottom of the page, click **Save Changes**; edX Studio will acknowledge your changes.

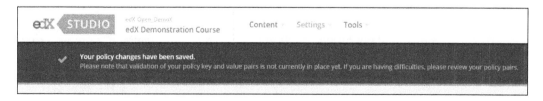

Once you've enabled content experiments, you need to specify at least one group configuration that defines how many groups of students will be a part of that experiment. After that you can create your content experiments.

 We will further discuss adding a content experiment into your edX course in *Chapter 5, Integrating the Curriculum*.

You can have any number of group configurations; simply select the group configuration to use. You might want to launch two different content experiments at different times. Consider the following two examples for this:

- **Content Experiment 1**: Here, students will watch a video or complete a reading assignment. You will then include problems designed to help them better understand which group learned more. For this content experiment, you need a group configuration that assigns your students to two groups.

- **Content Experiment 2**: You want to present the same question using four different types of problems. For this content experiment, you need a group configuration that assigns your students to four groups.

EdX assigns students to each group in one of the following four group configurations:

- **Dynamic**: Students are assigned to a group the first time they view a content experiment that uses the group configuration.

- **Random**: You have no control over which students are assigned to which group.

- **Evenly distributed**: New students are assigned to groups evenly. For example, if there are two groups, each group includes 50% of the students; if you have four groups, each group includes 25% of the students in the course.

- **Permanent**: Students remain in their assigned groups regardless of how many content experiments you launch with the same group configuration.

After you've enabled content experiments, you should see **Group Configurations** as an option when you click on the **Settings** menu. Once that is obtained as an available option, you can create and edit your group settings as desired. You will only notice something different when you create a new component of a unit by using the **Advanced Settings**. This functionality will be covered in *Chapter 6, Administering Your Course*.

Summary

In this chapter, you focused on developing exercises that encourage generative learning, which is a style of learning that helps them connect their existing knowledge with information that has been newly acquired. Likewise, we discussed an effective way to engage your students in ways that create a learning experience for everyone.

We also reviewed problem components and the different ways to challenge your students with interactive exercises. You were given examples of four problem types: general exercises and tools, image-based exercises and tools, multiple-choice exercises and tools, and STEM exercises and tools. You also touched on A/B split tests in conjunction with content experiments.

Now that you have your curriculum fully conceptualized, we move on to *Chapter 5, Integrating the Curriculum*, where you will learn to establish the structure of your course and integrate everything together. The chapter will also help you transition your course from idea to implementation.

5
Integrating the Curriculum

In their 1969 song *Come Together*, the Beatles sang "come together right now over me." Likewise, in this chapter, we will focus on bringing all the components of our class curriculum together into one cohesive edX course.

Chapter 1, Getting Started, walked you through setting up your Studio account and the framework for your first course. In *Chapter 2, Planning the Curriculum*, you learned how to develop curriculum. *Chapter 3, Producing Videos*, reviewed how to produce videos for your courses; and in *Chapter 4, Designing Exercises*, you were shown how to design exercises and assessments for your course.

We are now at the crossroads where these components converge. Assuming you've already followed the instructions in *Chapter 1, Getting Started*, and created your edX course shell, we will now put your pedagogical plans into production. Focused on creating components into which you can integrate your instructional materials, in this chapter, you will learn how to do the following:

- Establish your course outline
- Define course sections
- Include course subsections
- Input course units
- Develop course components
- Add pages to a course
- Upload files to a course
- Post updates and handouts
- Upload a course textbook
- Understand accessibility issues

Your course outline

In the *Creating your course* section of *Chapter 1, Getting Started*, you launched your edX course. Now, let's access the outline into which you will add your content:

1. Log in to Studio at `https://studio.edx.org/`.

 If you are developing a course on edX Edge, you have to log into Studio at `https://studio.edge.edx.org/`. If you are using Open edX, your URL will vary. For most examples, we will use the standard edX Studio login.

2. Select your course from those listed on the **My Courses** page.

3. View the **Course Outline** page, which displays when the course opens:

4. Select **Outline** in the **Content** menu to alternately view your **Course Outline**:

Now that you know how to access your course outline, let's review how to add a section, a subsection, and a unit. Each of these provides a place with a specific purpose, where you can integrate your course curriculum.

Course sections

A section is the top-level category of content in your edX course. It can represent a time period, a chapter in your textbook, a course concept, or another organizing principle. It might contain one or more subsections, each with any number of units.

Students see sections in the **Courseware** tab on the left-hand side of the screen (in the accordion). They can expand one section at a time to see its contents. Adding a section is simple and straightforward, as follows:

1. Log in to Studio at https://studio.edx.org/.

2. Click on the green **+ New section** button in the top-right corner:

3. Enter **New Section Name** and click on the blue **Save** button:

4. View the newly created section at the bottom of **Course Outline**:

5. Change the default section title from **New Section Name** by by typing a new section name and clicking on the blue **Save** button:

6. Change the section's release date and time by clicking on the clock icon in the **Release Date** area (it will turn blue when you hover over it):

 Release Time of edX courses is displayed in UTC, which stands for Coordinated Universal Time. You can convert the time of your time zone into UTC at `http://www.worldtimeserver.com/current_time_in_UTC.aspx`.

7. Change the **Release Day** and **Release Time in UTC** of the section, making note of the following points:

   ○ edX displays dates in the DD/MM/YYYY format

   ○ The default course start date is **1/1/2030**; if you don't change this when you create a new section, the release date will be **Unscheduled**

   ○ If you modify the course start date, the default release date when you create a new section will be the course start date

   ○ If the course start date is in the past, newly created sections immediately become visible to students

   ○ You can schedule release dates for sections and subsections

   ○ By default, a subsection inherits the release date of the section it is in, though you can change it to another date

The following shows a screenshot of the **Section Release Date**:

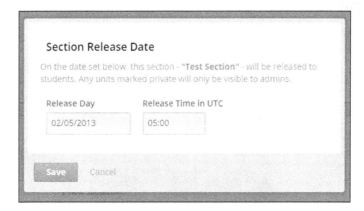

8. Move your section by hovering over the small dotted lines next to the shaded **Release Date** area until your cursor becomes a "move cursor" (shown in the following screenshot).

9. Click and hold your mouse button while dragging the section up or down the **Course Outline** to wherever you needed.

10. Release the button when the section is where you want it.

11. Delete your section by hovering over the trash can icon to the right of the **Release Date** area until it turns from gray to blue.

12. Click on it.

13. Then, click on the yellow button saying **Yes, delete this Section** when prompted:

Deleting a section deletes *all* the subsections and units within the section. Once deleted, you cannot restore the course content. If you are unsure whether or not you will use the content in your course but don't want to delete it, consider moving it into a section that you use as a staging area, but never publish.

Now that we've reviewed how to create and manage your course sections, let's move on to subsections.

Course subsections

Subsections are a subcategory within a section, corresponding to a lesson. Each lesson will contain a mixture of units housed within sections, and can represent a topic in your course, a course concept, a lesson plan, or some other organizing principle.

A series of subsections is called **learning sequences**. Students will see the subsections of your course in the **Courseware** tab beneath the expanded section. To add a subsection, perform these steps:

1. Identify the section in which you want to create a subsection, and hover over the green **+ New subsection** button at the bottom of that section.

2. Click on it when it turns blue:

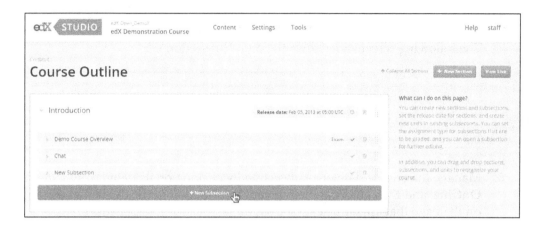

3. Change the default subsection title from **New subsection** by clicking on the section name and selecting the blue **Save** button:

4. Click on the gray checkmark on the right-hand side of the subsection title bar. Then select the type of assignments that will be contained in this subsection:

   ° **Exam**

   ° **Homework**

      °   **Not Graded**

 All problems in a subsection are graded and weighted as the same type; for different types of assignments, create a new subsection.

The following screenshot shows the New Subsection tab:

5.   Manage the release date of a subsection by clicking on its name from **Course Outline**, and then entering the relevant information in the fields that display on the page that appears next (shown in the following screenshot):

 You can also manually change the name of the subsection in the **Display Name** field. You can also add, edit, and manage **Units** from this interface.

6.   Move your subsection by hovering over the small dotted lines on the right-hand side of the subsection title bar until your cursor becomes a move cursor.

7.   Click and hold your mouse button while dragging the section up or down. Then release the button, as shown in the following screenshot:

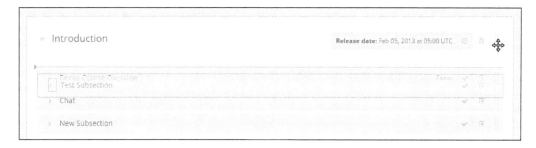

8. Delete your section by hovering over the trash can icon to the right of the shaded **Release Date** section until it turns from gray to blue.

9. Click on it (shown in the following screenshot).

10. Then click on the yellow button indicating **Yes, delete this Subsection** when prompted:

Now that we have created subsections, let's create units, where the core of your coursework will be accessed by students.

Course Units

Within a subsection, you will find a unit containing at least one component, including a content experiment, HTML, problems, discussions, and videos. Students will see a unit as a single page. In addition, a unit is not represented in the course accordion, but instead it appears in the course ribbon at the top of each unit.

In the following screenshot, the unit consists of the right two thirds of the interface, with the **Lesson 2: Let's Get Interactive** headline. Note that the icon for three other units is in the ribbon above the unit:

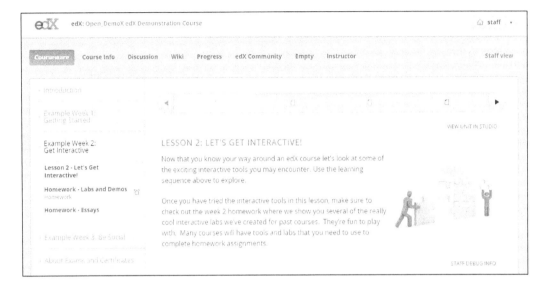

Create a unit, either from the course outline or in the same subsection, as follows:

1. Click on the blue **+ New Unit** button at the bottom of the section in which you want the unit to appear (shown in the following screenshot).

2. Create a unit from **Course Outline**.

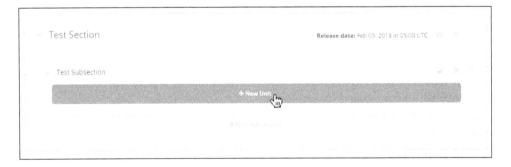

3. Create a unit in the same subsection by clicking on the blue **+ New Unit** button in the **Unit Location** panel; the new unit displays automatically (shown in the following image).

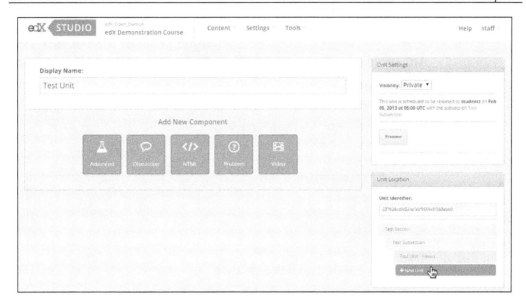

4. Change the default unit title of your newly created unit from **New Unit** to anything of your choice. Your changes will be automatically saved:

 If the value for the **advanced_modules Policy Key** is empty list (for example, [ ]) the **Advanced** icon might not appear here as an option.

5. Add one of these five components to your unit (shown in the following screenshot):
    ◦ **Advanced**
    ◦ **Discussion**
    ◦ **HTML**
    ◦ **Problem**
    ◦ **Video**

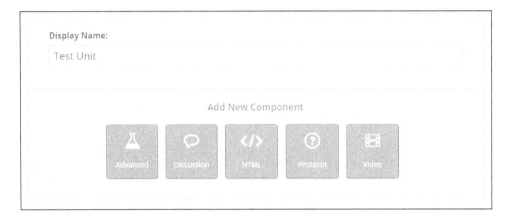

6. Change the order in which your units appear in your subsection by hovering over the small dotted lines on the right-hand side of the unit title bar until your cursor becomes a move cursor.

7. Click and hold your mouse button while dragging the section up or down, and then release the button, as shown in the following screenshot:

8. Publish your unit by selecting **Public** from the drop-down menu in the **Unit Settings** panel. This makes it viewable to students once the unit is released as per the indicated schedule (shown in the following screenshot).

 If you make a unit **Public** but the unit is not released, the content will not be visible to students. You can also click on **Preview** to see how your unit will appear to your students once it is live.

9. Open the editing function of your published (public) unit by clicking on **edit a draft** in the **Unit Settings** panel:

10. Once the editing function is open, you can make any necessary changes to your unit, including adding, editing, or deleting components. You can also delete the current draft on which you are working, preview your changes, or view the live version of the unit, as shown in the following screenshot.

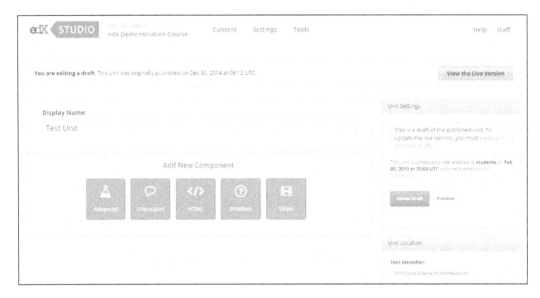

11. Delete your unit by hovering over the trash can icon on the right-hand side of the unit bar until it turns from gray to blue. Then click on it, as shown in the following screenshot:

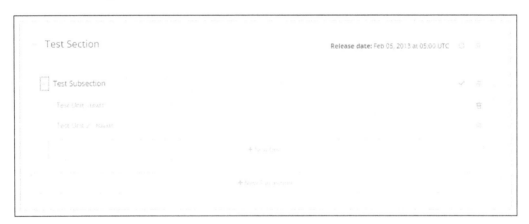

12. Click on the yellow button saying **Yes, delete this unit**, when prompted:

Now that you have gained a better understanding about creating units, let's explore the various types of components that are available for your units. This was also reviewed briefly in the *Characteristics of your course* section of *Chapter 1, Getting Started*.

Course components

Components are the area in a unit that contains your course content; they are represented by an icon in that unit's ribbon. There are five types of content you can add to your course:

- **Discussion components**: This is where you and your students can go to add posts, comments, and responses to a question. Discussions added to an individual unit appear in the course's **Discussion Forum**. For additional information about discussion components, refer to the *Discussion components* section. You can also read the *Course discussions* section of *Chapter 7, Facilitating Your Course*, for more detailed instructions.

- **HTML components**: This is used to add information to a unit, including text, lists, links, and images. You can import LaTeX code here and insert hand-coded content (or any content that you've programmed using a WYSIWYG editor). For additional information about HTML components, refer to the *HTML components* section.

 WYSIWYG is an acronym for *What You See Is What You Get*. Pronounced "wihzeewig," it refers to HTML editing software that visually represents how the code of a website looks to the human eye (as opposed to hand-coding, which does not). For more information on this, read the article *WYSIWYG* at http://techterms.com/definition/wysiwyg.

- **Problem components**: You can add interactive, automatically graded exercises to your course with this component. There are many types of problems you can design, depending on the learning objectives of your course. For additional information about adding problem components, refer to the *Exercises and tools* section of *Chapter 4, Designing Exercises*.

- **Video**: Create videos of lectures and add them to your course, along with other components, to promote active learning. Adding a video to your course has several steps, which were previously reviewed in *Chapter 3, Producing Videos*. edX is designed to stream videos uploaded to YouTube, but you can also create files of any video available for students to download in several different formats. For additional information about video components, refer to the *Video components* section.

Advanced components

Adding an **Advanced Component** lets you include a content experiment in your course. As you first learned in the *Content experiments* section of *Chapter 4, Designing Exercises*, with this option activated, you can use A/B split tests to share different course content with groups of students. Having also learned how to enable content experiments in *Chapter 4, Designing Exercises*, you can now go ahead and add an advanced component to your course:

1. Log in to Studio at `https://studio.edx.org/`.

2. Select your course from your list of **My Courses**:

3. Click on the gray, right-facing arrow in the bar, which represents the intended subsection:

4. Click on the white **+ New Unit** bar when it turns blue.

5. Click on the green **Advanced** button under **Add a New Component**:

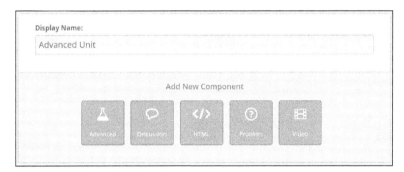

6. Select **Content Experiment**:

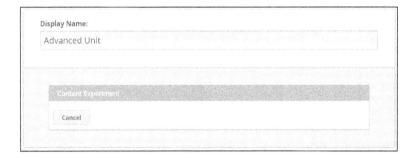

7. Select the yellow text that reads **Select a Group Configuration** to associate the content experiment with a group configuration. This will open the **Editing** window.

8. Hover over the **EDIT** link until it turns blue, and click on it to open the editing window:

9. Edit the **Display Name** of the **Content Experiment**, if necessary.

 Note the **Clear** icon to the right of the **Display Name** field. Clicking on it reverses any changes you made to the field. Look for it in other fields.

10. Toggle the **Group Configuration** drop-down menu to define how users are grouped for this content experiment:

 Changing the group configuration of a student-visible experiment will impact the experiment data.

11. Hover over the **duplicate** icon so that it turns blue, and click on it to duplicate the content experiment:

12. Hover over the **trash can** icon so that it turns blue, and click on it to delete the content experiment:

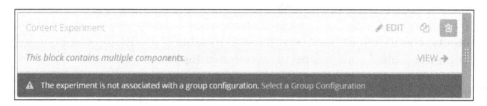

13. Click on the yellow **Yes, delete this component** button to delete the content experiment; click on **Cancel** to leave it as is:

14. Hover over the **VIEW** link until it turns blue to view how the content experiment will look to a student:

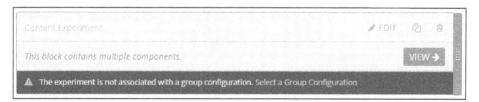

15. Hover over the vertical sidebar on the right-hand side of the **Content Experiment** until it turns blue. Drag it vertically or horizontally, if needed, to reposition it within the **Unit**:

Discussion components

Discussion components give students an opportunity to engage with each other about a topic related to the course curriculum, while helping create a sense of community. Discussion topics that you create by adding discussion components to your course are called content-specific discussion topics.

 You are encouraged to add an HTML component before each discussion component to introduce the topic that you want your students to discuss. The discussion component itself doesn't contain any text and, as a result, could be easy for learners to overlook.

When you are ready to add a discussion component to your course, perform these steps:

1. Log in to Studio at `https://studio.edx.org/`.

2. Select your course from your list of **My Courses**.

3. Click on the gray, right-facing arrow in the bar representing the intended subsection:

4. Click on the white **+ New Unit** bar when it turns blue:

5. Click on the green **Discussion** button under **Add a New Component**:

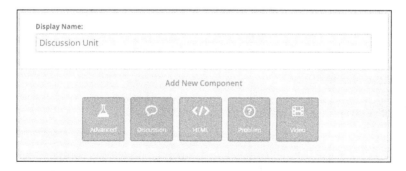

6. Hover over the **EDIT** link until it turns blue, and click on it to open the editing window:

7. Follow the guidelines in the editor to fill in the **Category**, **Display Name**, and **Subcategory** fields:

> The value in the **Display Name** field identifies the discussion in the course content. The values in the **Category** and **Subcategory** fields appear in the list of discussion topics on the **Discussion** tab. Each **Category/Subcategory** pair for the discussion topics in your course must be unique.

8. Click on the blue **Save** button.

> Always use the preceding steps to create a discussion component; do not create discussion topics using the **Duplicate** button in Studio. Duplicated discussion components result in discussion topics containing the same conversations, even if users post in different discussions.

9. Navigate to your live course.

10. Click on **Discussion**.

11. View the discussion you added, as shown in the following screenshot:

 You cannot see the category and subcategory names of discussion components that you created on the **Discussion** tab until after the course starts and the unit is released.

HTML components

To learn about working with HTML components in edX, visit `http://edx.readthedocs.org/projects/edx-partner-course-staff/en/latest/creating_content/create_html_component.html?highlight=wysiwyg`

Text:

1. Log in to Studio at `https://studio.edx.org/`.

2. Select your course from your list of **My Courses**.

3. Click on the gray, right-facing arrow in the bar representing the intended subsection:

4. Click on the white **+ New Unit** bar when it turns blue:

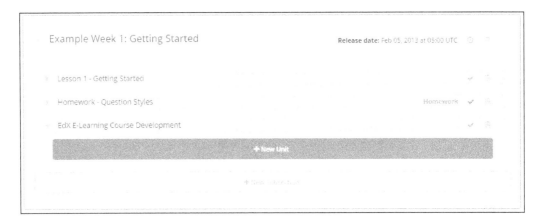

5. Click on the green **HTML** button under **Add a New Component**:

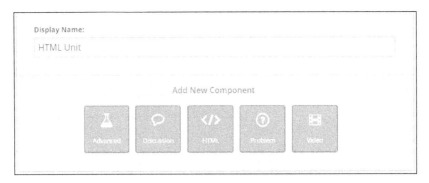

6. Select any one from the seven available component templates: **Text,
    Announcement, Anonymous User ID, Full Screen Image, IFrame, Raw
    HTML**, and **Zoning Image**.

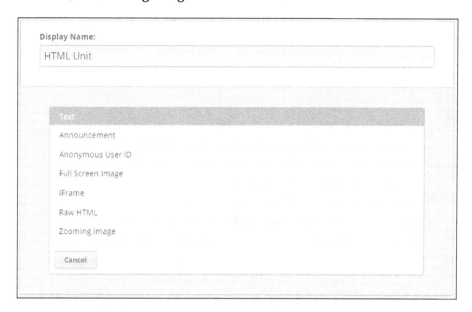

 The remainder of these instructions will feature the use the **Text**
template for the example.

7. Hover over the **EDIT** link until it turns blue, and click on it to open the
    editing window for the **Text** component:

8. Enter and format your content in the editor window, as shown in the following screenshot:

9. Click on **Settings** in the top-right corner of the component editor.

10. Enter text in the **Display Name** field.

 The **Display Name** field appears in the horizontal navigation at the top of the page.

11. Toggle the **Editor** drop-down menu to indicate **Visual** or **Raw**:

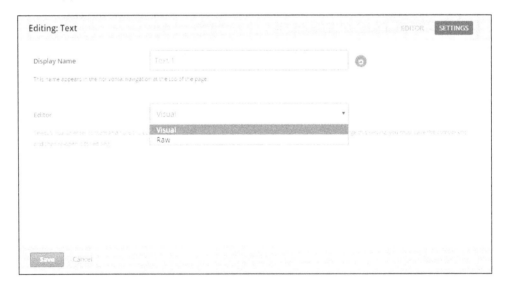

Select **Visual** to enter the content and have the editor automatically create the HTML. You can learn more about this editor at http://edx.readthedocs.org/projects/edx-partner-course-staff/en/latest/creating_content/create_html_component.html?highlight=wysiwyg#the-visual-editor. Select **Raw** to edit HTML directly. If you change this setting, you must save the component and reopen it for editing. You can learn more about this editor at http://edx.readthedocs.org/projects/edx-partner-course-staff/en/latest/creating_content/create_html_component.html?highlight=wysiwyg#the-raw-html-editor.

12. Click on the blue **Save** button or on **Cancel**:

When using the **Visual** editor, you can also perform the following functions. Links are provided to instructions for each function in the online resource *Building and Running an edX Course*:

- *Add a Link in an HTML Component*:
  http://edx.readthedocs.org/projects/edx-partner-course-staff/en/latest/creating_content/create_html_component.html?highlight=wysiwyg#add-a-link-in-an-html-component

- *Add an Image to an HTML Component*:
  http://edx.readthedocs.org/projects/edx-partner-course-staff/en/latest/creating_content/create_html_component.html?highlight=wysiwyg#add-an-image-to-an-html-component

- *Import LaTeX Code into an HTML Component*:
  http://edx.readthedocs.org/projects/edx-partner-course-staff/en/latest/creating_content/create_html_component.html?highlight=wysiwyg#import-latex-code-into-an-html-component

Problem components

edX's problem components let you to add interactive, automatically graded exercises to your course. One of edX's strengths is the interactivity of its exercises and the multitude of options you have. However, because creating problem components is such an essential element to your course, it is thoroughly explained in *Chapter 4, Designing Exercises*.

Video components

Now, let's highlight how to add, edit, and delete a video component from your course; the steps here are similar to those for the other components, but since videos are the core of your curriculum, we will focus on them to best serve the goals of this book. Given the extensive instructions for problem components in *Chapter 4, Designing Exercises*, you should already have an understanding of this functionality:

1. Log in to Studio at `https://studio.edx.org/`.

2. Select your course from your list of **My Courses**.

3. Click on the gray, right-facing arrow in the bar representing the intended subsection:

4. Click on the white **+ New Unit** bar when it turns blue:

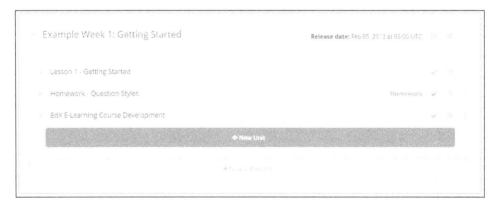

5. Click on the green **Video** button under **Add a New Component**:

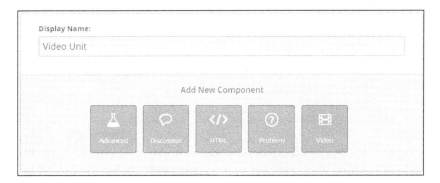

6. Hover over the **EDIT** link until it turns blue, and click on it to open the editing window for the **Video** component:

7.   Enter in the **Component Display Name** field the name that you want students to see when they hover their mouse over the unit in the course ribbon. This text will also serve as a header for the video:

8.   Enter the link to the video in the **Default Video URL** field. Click on **+ Add URLs for additional versions** if you have alternate versions of your video to share:

9.   Select an option next to **Default Timed Transcript**.

If the video has a transcript compatible with edX, you will see a green checkmark with the words **Timed Transcript Found**. If the video does not, you will see the following options:

10. Click on the blue **Import YouTube Transcript** button to import the default transcript from YouTube.

11. Click on the blue **Upload New Transcript** button to use a new transcript— and not the default YouTube version that edX found.

 For more information about transcripts for your videos, refer to the *Transcripts for your videos* section in *Chapter 3, Producing Videos*.

Advanced video options

Having addressed the basic video options, let's review the advanced functions:

1. Click on the **ADVANCED** link to edit the advanced options for your video:

2. Review the **Component Display Name** field. This is the name that students see; it appears in the course ribbon and as a header for the video:

3. Update the **Default Timed Transcript** field. This indicates the YouTube ID of the default (English) transcript for the video. It is pulled from the **Default Timed Transcript** field in the **BASIC** tab:

4. Choose the **Download Transcript Allowed** option. Toggle the drop-down menu to **True** to allow students to download the timed transcript as a `.srt` or `.txt` file, or choose **False** to prevent this:

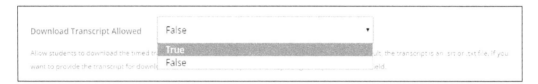

5. Enter **Downloadable Transcript URL**. Here, you need to indicate the link where a transcript for the video is available for download:

6. Choose the **Show Transcript** option. Toggle the drop-down menu to **True** to make the transcript appear, or **False** to prevent it from appearing:

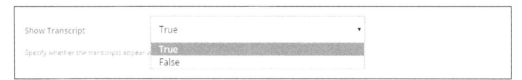

7. Select **Transcript Language**. Hover over the white **+ Add** button until it turns blue, and then click on it:

8. Choose the language of your transcript from the drop-down menu:

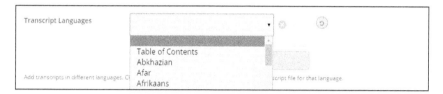

9. Next, hover over the white **+ Upload** button until it turns blue, and click on it:

10. Select the gray **Choose File** button in the **Upload translation** pop-up window:

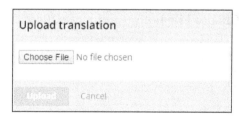

11. Locate the proper `.srt` file, and click on the gray **Open** button to attach it:

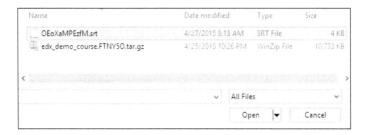

12. Click on the blue **Upload** button:

13. Complete the **Upload Handout** option.

14. Hover over the white **+ Upload** button until it turns blue, and click on it:

15. Select the gray **Choose File** button and locate the file:

16. Click on the gray **Open** button to attach it:

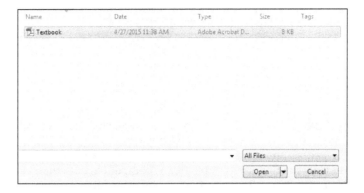

17. Click on the blue **Upload** button:

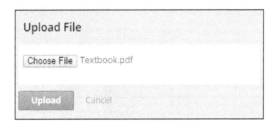

18. Indicate the **Video Download Allowed** option:

 Selecting **True** allows students to download versions of this video in different formats if they cannot use the edX video player or do not have access to YouTube. You must add at least one non-YouTube URL in the **Video File URLs** field.

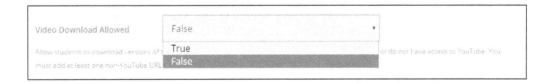

19. Add the **Video File URLs**:

Include the URL or URLs where you've posted non-YouTube versions of the video. Each URL must end in .mpeg, .mp4, .ogg, or .webm, and it cannot be a YouTube URL. Students will be able to view the first listed video that is compatible with their computer. Selecting **True** allows students to download these videos.

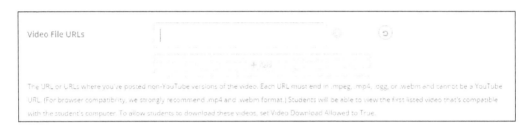

20. Enter **Video Start Time**:

Video Start Time is the time you want the video to start from if you don't want the entire video to play. While the **Video Stop Time** should be the time you want the video to stop at if you don't want the entire video to play. Format the time as HH:MM:SS; the maximum value is 23:59:59.

21. Enter **Video Stop Time**:

22. Enter **YouTube ID** (for the normal speed video):

23. Enter **YouTube ID for .75x speed**:

24. Enter **YouTube ID for 1.25x speed**:

25. Enter **YouTube ID for 1.5x speed**:

 The previous four fields are optional fields that you have to complete for older browsers.

26. Click on the blue **Save** button when you're done; or click on **Cancel**:

Moving a video component

Hover over the vertical sidebar on the right-hand side of the video component until it turns blue. Then drag it vertically or horizontally, if needed, to reposition it within the **Unit**:

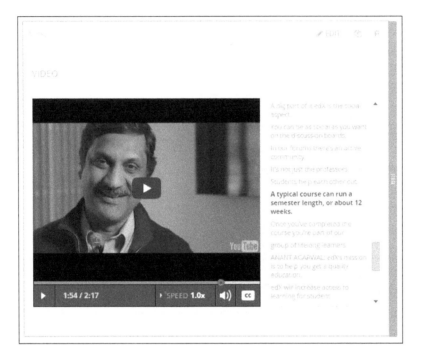

Deleting a video component

1. Hover over the trash can icon until it turns blue, and click on it to delete the video component:

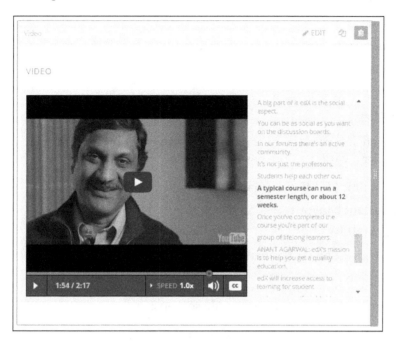

2. Click on the yellow **Yes, delete this component** button; or you can click on **Cancel**:

Course pages

By default, your course has the following pages listed, each of which appears in your course's navigation bar:

- **Courseware**
- **Course Info**
- **Discussion**
- **Wiki**
- **Progress**

You cannot rename, reorder, or remove these pages. You can, however, add pages to your course for a variety of purposes such as:

- A dynamic HTML calendar
- An instant hangout
- Course slides
- A Google calendar (embedding the code for it)
- A grading policy

To add a page to your course, perform these steps:

1. Select **Pages** from the **Content** menu:

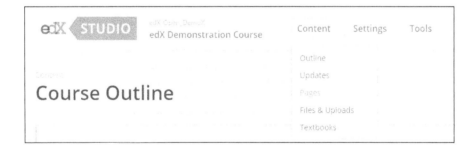

2. Click on the green **+ New Page** button in the top-right corner of your page or the green **+ Add New Page** button under the list of pages. This will add a page with the title **Empty** to the list:

3. Hover over the **EDIT** icon for the page you wish to edit until it turns blue, and then click on it. This will open the HTML editor:

4. Make any additions, edits, or deletions that you want to the HTML page:

5. Click on **Settings** to edit the **Display Name**. The display name is the name of the page that will be visible to the students of the course:

6. Click on the blue **Save** button.
7. To hide the **Wiki** page or make it viewable, click on the eye icon:

8. Move a page by hovering over the element handle on the right side of the page row until the mouse pointer changes to a four-headed arrow. Then, click and drag the page to the location you want:

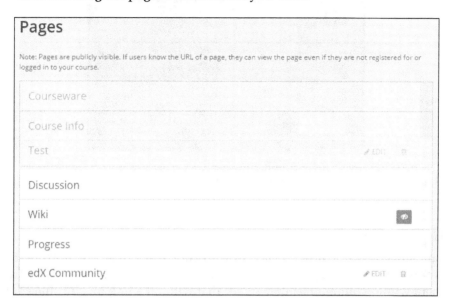

9. Delete a page by clicking on the trash can icon in the row for that page:

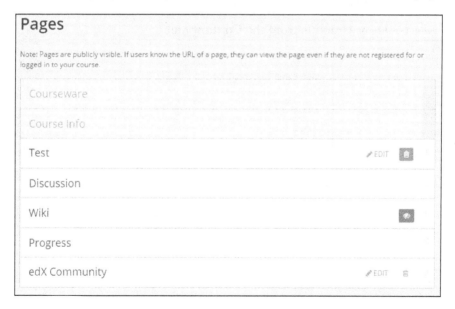

10. Click on the yellow **OK** button when you are asked to confirm the page deletion:

We will now move on to discuss adding files to your course.

Course files

To use any images or documents, such as your course syllabus, you must first upload the files from the **Files & Uploads** page. Then you link to the uploaded files from a component within your course. Remember that without a link to a file, the students can't see it.

Here's how to upload a file for your course:

1. Select **Files & Uploads** from the **Content** menu:

2. Click on the green **+ Upload New File** button:

 Here's a warning: if you upload a file that has the same name as an existing course file, the original file will be overwritten without warning.

3. Click on the blue **Choose File** button in the **Upload New File** dialog box:

4. Select one or more files to upload in the **Open** dialog box, and click on **Open**.

5. Click on the blue **Load Another File** button, and repeat the previous step to upload additional files:

6. Click on the **X** sign in the top-right corner to close the dialog box.

7. Navigate through all the uploaded files by using the navigational arrows at the top of the **Files & Uploads** page:

8. Skip to a specific page number or navigate to the previous or next page by using the arrow keys at the bottom of the **Files & Uploads** page:

9. To ensure that those not in your class cannot view a file, click on the lock icon:

 By default, anyone can access a file you've uploaded if they know the URL — even people who are not enrolled in your class.

10. Delete a file by clicking on the **X** icon, which is located next to the file:

11. Click on **Delete** when you are asked to confirm the file deletion:

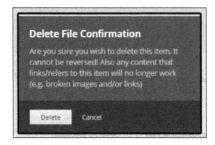

After you have uploaded a file, you can add a link to it from a component, a course update, or the course handouts, using the links generated on the **Files & Uploads** page. The **Studio URL** and **Web URL** are listed on the **Files & Uploads** page. To provide a link to the file or image from outside the course, use **Web URL**. Now, we will move on to discussing adding updates and handouts.

Updates and Handouts

Add course updates and handouts to your course to ensure that students are informed about class activities and have all the necessary course materials. Students can see the course updates and handouts in the **Course Info** tab in your course.

Course Updates

Communication is critical to any class, especially when that class is online— and even more so when it is a MOOC. Adding an update is relatively simple and straightforward:

1. Select **Updates** from the **Content** menu:

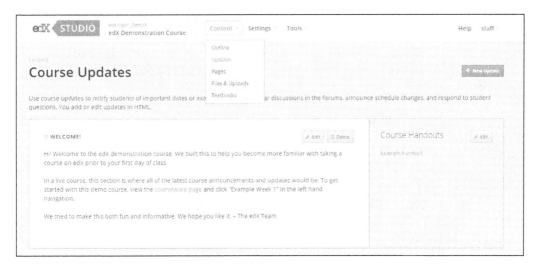

2. Click on the green **+ New Update** button.
3. Enter your update in the HTML editor that opens.
4. Click on the blue **Save** button when you are done:

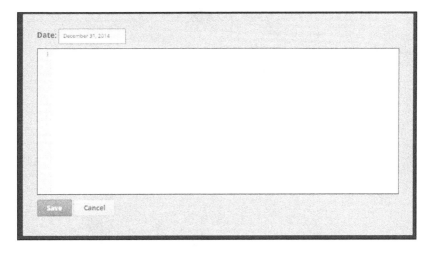

Course Handouts

Just as updating your students is essential for the effective operation of your edX course, it is also important to provide them with any materials needed to complete the coursework. Whether you are distributing a textbook for your course or a worksheet, you can perform these steps to add a handout to your course:

1. Select **Updates** from the **Content** menu:

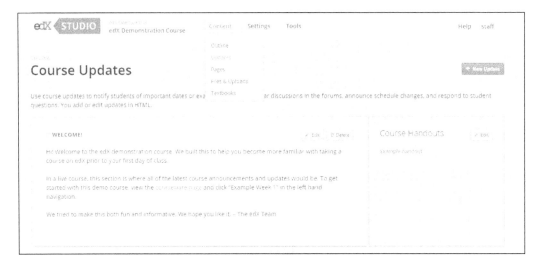

2. Click on **Edit** in the **Course Handouts** panel:

3. Edit the HTML to include links to the files you've already uploaded (see the previous *Course files* section for a refresher, if necessary):

4. Click on the blue **Save** button when you're done.

Your course might or might not have a PDF textbook, but if you do, it's important to make it available for your students. In the next section, we will see how to upload a PDF textbook to your edX course.

PDF textbooks

If your course uses a textbook, you can add a PDF version of it for students to download and use. Each textbook that you add is displayed to students as a tab in the course navigation bar.

 To avoid forcing your students to download one large file, it is recommended that you upload a separate PDF file for each chapter of your textbook.

1. Select **Textbooks** from the **Content** menu:

2. Click on the green **+ New Textbook** button:

3. Enter **Textbook Name** and **Chapter Name**.

4. Add a PDF file from your computer by clicking on the **Upload PDF** button. Follow the prompts to upload your file as shown in the following screenshot:

 It's possible that you could encounter errors when uploading a PDF file with Firefox; if that is the case, you should try again, using Google Chrome.

5. Hover your mouse over the **+ Add a Chapter** bar to add more chapters.

6. Click on it when it turns blue.

7. Repeat the preceding steps as many times as needed as shown:

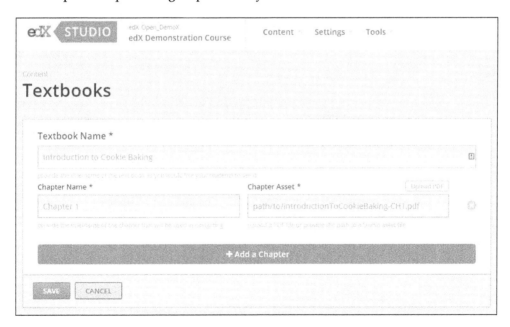

8. Click on the blue **Save** button when you are done.

With your textbook added to your course and everything ready to go, let's ensure that all of your content is accessible to students with disabilities.

Accessibility issues

It's likely that a notable percentage of your students will have some form of disability. If you are teaching within the United States, your students are protected by the Americans with Disabilities Act (ADA). Even if you are outside America, you should stay mindful about students who might have unique challenges.

According to a U.S. Census Bureau report titled *Americans with Disabilities: 2010*, nearly 60 million people – 19 percent of the population of the United States – have some form of disability, with more than half of them indicating that it was severe. According to the United Nations, roughly 15 percent of the world's population – an estimated 1 billion people – lives with disabilities.

Given these significant statistics, when you integrate your curriculum into your edX course, it's important to remain mindful of students with special needs.

 Explore the *Guidelines for Creating Accessible Content* section of the online edX document *Building and Running an EdX Course* at `http://edx.readthedocs.org/projects/edx-partner-course-staff/en/latest/getting_started/accessibility.html`.

You might also find reviewing these resources and articles helpful as you endeavor to develop a curriculum that is inclusive of individuals with disabilities:

- *10 Free Web-Based Web Site Accessibility Evaluation Tools*: `http://usabilitygeek.com/10-free-web-based-web-site-accessibility-evaluation-tools/`

- *ADA Compliance Is a 'Major Vulnerability' for Online Programs*: `http://chronicle.com/blogs/wiredcampus/ada-compliance-a-major-vulnerability-for-online-programs/28136`

- *Best Practices* under ADA Section 508: `http://www.section508.gov/best-practices`

- *Americans with Disabilities Act (ADA) and Accessible Online Video Requirements*: `http://www.3playmedia.com/2013/06/13/the-americans-disability-act-ada-accessible-online-video-requirements/`

- *Creating ADA-Compliant Course Sites: An Online Training Program*: `http://www.educause.edu/annual-conference/2013/creating-ada-compliant-course-sites-online-training-program`

- *E-learning and disability: accessibility as a contribute to inclusion*:
  `http://www.academia.edu/2061905/E_learning_and_disability_`
  `accessibility_as_a_contribute_to_inclusion`

- *Hidden Disabilities: Is Your e-Learning Fully Section 508 Compliant?*:
  `http://www.learningsolutionsmag.com/articles/249/hidden-`
  `disabilities-is-your-e-learning-fully-section-508-compliant`

- *Higher Ed Accessibility Lawsuits*:
  `http://blog.lib.umn.edu/itsshelp/news/2013/10/higher-ed-`
  `accessibility-lawsuits.html`

- *Improve Accessibility in Tomorrow's Online Courses by Leveraging Yesterday's Techniques*:
  `http://www.facultyfocus.com/articles/online-education/improve-`
  `accessibility-tomorrows-online-courses-leveraging-yesterdays-`
  `techniques/`

- *Information and Technical Assistance on the Americans with Disabilities Act*:
  `http://www.ada.gov`

Summary

In this chapter, we focused on creating components where your curriculum can converge. We reviewed how to integrate your existing curriculum and provide places to include other materials to enrich your students' learning experiences.

We also walked through how to establish your course outline, define course sections, include course subsections, input course units, develop course components, add pages, upload files, post updates and handouts, upload PDF textbooks, and consider accessibility issues.

With the stage set, the operation of your edX course can now commence. Aimed at the backend functionality, *Chapter 6, Administering Your Course*, will teach you how to manage the administrative functions of your course for a smooth and successful educational experience for your students.

6

Administering Your Course

"If you can't do, teach. If you can't teach, administrate."

So says a popular idiom, but while administrators often bear the brunt of your angst as an educator, their responsibilities outside of your classroom counterbalance yours inside it. Similarly, your energetic interaction during class is complemented by your administrative preparation before school starts.

This is similar to the debate between leadership and management. Leadership is an elusive concept to comprehend and a harder idea to implement, but a good leader can make a great impact. Yet, leadership cannot succeed in a vacuum.

Leadership might ignite a fire, but effective management keeps it burning. The late Warren Bennis, former distinguished professor of business administration at the University of Southern California, shared this concept: "Leadership is the capacity to translate vision into reality."

Your task is to translate your curriculum into an engaging educational experience. That's where this chapter comes in: focused on the backend functional aspects of your course in this chapter, we will discuss the best practices with which you can:

- Establish a grading policy
- Control content visibility
- Include student cohorts
- Tackle beta testing
- Export and import a course
- Review edX resources
- Launch a course

Grading policy

Your grading policy establishes the point ranges for each letter grade and defines the minimum for passing grades. Your course can be pass/fail, or it can have the letter grades of A through F. To create a grading policy for your class, follow these steps:

1. Select **Grading** from the **Settings** menu.

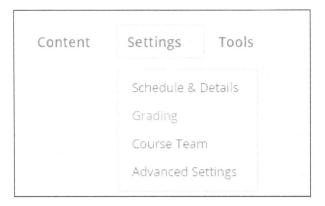

2. View the default Pass/Fail grade scale in the **Overall Grade Range** section.

3. Click on the **+** button to add a grade. Clicking the button will change the scale from pass/fail to a range of letter grade options.

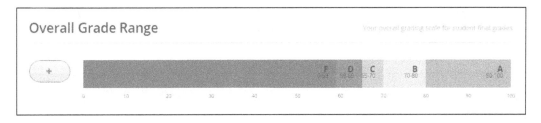

4. Click on the yellow **Save Changes** button when you are done with making the changes.

5. Change the grade range by moving the cursor onto the line that divides two grades.

6. Click and drag the line to the left or right to adjust the range for each letter grade. Release the mouse button when the line is where you want it.

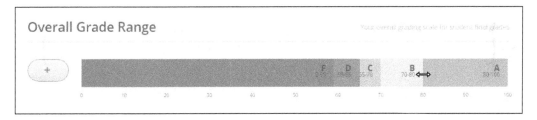

7. Change the name of the grade by double-clicking on the current name and then typing your desired new name for that specific grade.

For example, if you want to change the original grade name of Pass, you must double-click on the word Pass, and then type whatever you want to replace the name. However, you cannot change F or Fail.

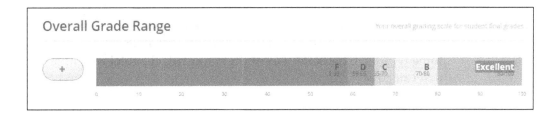

8. Remove a grade by moving the cursor onto the grade and clicking on the **Remove** link above the grade.

[ You cannot remove F or A from the grade range.]

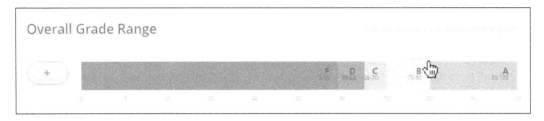

9. Extend the due dates for your students by entering a value in the **Hours:Minutes** format in the **Grace Period on Deadline** field in the **Grading Rules & Policies** section.

[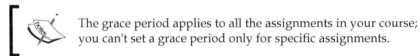 The grace period applies to all the assignments in your course; you can't set a grace period only for specific assignments.]

10. Create a new assignment type by clicking on the green **+ New Assignment Type** button and configuring the fields explained. You must create assignment types for your course, and indicate the weight they have towards the student's total grade; all the assignments must add up to 100 percent:

    ○ **Assignment Type Name**: This indicates the category of the assignment; this name is visible to students. All assignments of the same type have the same contribution towards the total weight of that category.

For example, a homework assignment with 10 problems is worth the same percentage as a homework assignment with 20 problems.

- ° **Abbreviation**: This is the short name of an assignment that appears in a student's **Progress** tab. Think of it as a shorthand code.
- ° **Weight of Total Grade**: The assignments of a type collectively account for the percent value set in **Weight of Total Grade**.

 Make sure that you don't include the percent sign (%) in this field.

- ° **Total Number**: The number of assignments of a specific type that you plan to include in your course.
- ° **Number of Droppable**: The number of assignments of a specific type that the grader can drop, starting with the lowest scored assignments.

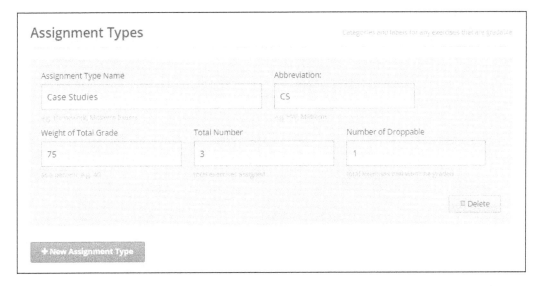

11. Indicate the **Assignment Type Name** and **Due Date** for a subsection by designating a subsection as a graded assignment. This is done by setting the assignment type for subsections that contain problems that are to be graded.

Each subsection that contains problems to be graded can include only one assignment type. You can also create problems in Studio without specifying that the subsection is an assignment type, but such problems do not count toward a student's grade.

12. See a student's view of their problem scores and the percentage of the course they've completed, by logging in to the live course and clicking on the red **Staff view** link in the top-right corner of the edX interface, switching it to a green **Student view** link.

13. Click on **Progress** in the top navigation bar.

Content visibility

It is important to manage the pace your students follow to complete your course. One way to do this is by controlling which content is visible throughout the class. You can control content visibility through the following means:

- **Release dates**: By default, a subsection has the same release date as the section in which it is located, but you can change the date. Additionally, a published unit will not be displayed until the scheduled release date. If a section and a subsection have different release dates, a published unit will not appear as published until both the dates have passed by.

> You can preview a course before it releases by viewing the live course (see step 12 in the *Grading policy* section for instructions on accessing content as a staff member or student).

- **Unit publishing status**: Publishing a unit makes it visible to students. They will see the most recently published version of a unit when the section and subsection it is in are released. Students will not see units that are unpublished, just as they won't see changes made to units or components of units that have not been published. This enables you to edit unpublished units without affecting the student experience.

> Refer to *Chapter 5, Integrating the Curriculum*, for additional details about publishing the content of your course.

- **Content hidden from students**: If you have a need to restrict access to some content, you can hide it from your students' view, regardless of its release and publishing status. You can hide content at three different levels: sections, subsections, and units.

> When you make content that was previously hidden visible again, all of that content might not become visible. For example, if you have hidden a child subsection or unit, it will stay hidden. Additionally, unpublished units remain unpublished, just as changes to unpublished units remain unpublished.

- **Content groups**: Use cohorts to designate particular components in your course as visible only to specific groups of students.

Student cohorts

Setting up cohorts in a course allows you to create smaller groups of students. This is especially useful in very large courses. Different cohorts of students can have different experiences, including discussions that are limited to members of the same cohort.

A student must be assigned to one cohort, and that student must remain in the same cohort for the duration of a class.

If you decide to configure cohorts in your course, first define a set of cohorts to reflect communities of students, and then select a strategy for assigning students to one of the cohorts you created. Your strategy options include the following:

- **Automated assignment**: This is useful when you have very large enrollment in your courses. The first time a student views the course's **Discussion** page (or any content-specific discussion topic), they are randomly assigned to an automated cohort.

> Automated cohorts work best if they have at least 200 members and no more than 500 members. Notably, for every 10,000 students enrolled, 200 to 400 will typically stay active in the discussions. So, to determine how many automated cohorts to create, divide the estimated total enrollment of the course by 10,000. Then use that result as the number of necessary automated cohorts. Automated cohorts are not useful when the enrollment for a course is fewer than 10,000 students.

- **Manual assignment**: In SPOCs and courses with small- to medium-sized enrollments, you can use known similarities to determine cohorts (for example, students who are from the same company). You might choose this enrollment strategy because students with characteristics in common are more likely to share ideas with each other, and they will possibly be in a better situation to apply what they learned in class to their shared environment outside the class. To do this, you will need to enable the cohort feature and create a manual cohort for each cohort. You will then assign a student to one of the manual cohorts you just created. Every student who enrolls must be assigned to a cohort; to ensure that this happens, create a single automated cohort, as described for the hybrid assignment strategy.

> If you don't create an automated cohort, the system automatically creates a default cohort and assigns students to it if necessary.

- **Hybrid assignment**: You may also use a hybrid of the two aforementioned automated and manual strategies. First, you need to identify the characteristics that define the existing cohorts in the student body, and decide whether you want the rest of the students in the course to be divided into their own, similarly-sized cohorts or another cohort. After you enable the cohort, create a manual cohort for each cohort you identified and assign students to each. You also must set up automated cohorts for the other students in the course, or rely on the default.

> Students not assigned to a manual cohort are automatically assigned to an automated cohort or a default cohort when they first view the **Discussion** page or a discussion topic. For best results with this strategy, complete all manual assignments before the course begins.

- **Default assignment**: If you have cohorts enabled in your course, then every student must be assigned to a cohort. If you have not created at least one automated assignment cohort by the time the first student accesses your course, the system will automatically create a default cohort and assign that student to it.

> Students assigned to the default cohort see cohort name **Default Group** in discussion posts. If you want students to see a different cohort name, you can add an automated cohort with the name that you prefer.

After you've selected a strategy, complete these configuration steps:

1. Enable cohorts by opening the course in Studio and selecting **Settings** and then **Advanced Settings**.

2. Place your cursor between the pair of braces in the **Cohort Configuration** field, and type `"cohorted": true`.

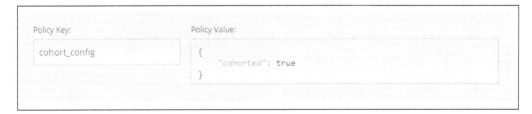

3. Click on the yellow **Save Changes** button.

[Studio reformats the `name:value` pair you enter and indents it on a new line.]

4. Chose one of the four cohort methods mentioned above: automated, manual, hybrid, and default.

[Optionally, you can also identify the discussion topics that you want to be divided by cohort.]

Whichever strategy you use, remember that students can see the name of the cohort to which they are assigned. The **This post is visible only to {cohort name}** message appears with every post in discussion topics that are divided into cohorts.

Assigning cohorts automatically

To implement the automated assignment strategy, follow these steps:

1. Open your course in Studio.

2. Select **Settings** and then **Advanced Settings**.

3. Define auto-cohorts in the **Cohort Configuration** advanced setting field (if you are using either the automated or hybrid assignment strategy for your course).

4. Place your cursor after the opening brace character, {, in the **Cohort Configuration** field.

5. Press *Enter*.

6. Define the `"auto_cohort_groups"`: policy key on the new line, followed by one or more cohort names enclosed within quotation marks (" "), separating the quoted name values with commas and enclosing all sets of auto-cohort names in square brackets, [and].

7. Type a comma after the closing square bracket,], making sure that you include a comma to separate each of the policy keys that you define. Your entry should resemble what is shown in the following screenshot:

Policy Key: Policy Value:

```
cohort_config                        {
                                        "auto_cohort_groups": [
                                            "Example Cohort Name A",
                                            "Example Cohort Name B",
                                            "Example Cohort Name C"
                                        ],
                                          "cohorted": true
                                     }
```

8. Click on the yellow **Save Changes** button.

9. Scroll back to the **Cohort Configuration** field to verify that your entry was saved.

 Entries that do not contain all the required punctuation characters revert to the previous value when you save; no warning is presented.

After you've made this change, a student not assigned to a cohort will be randomly assigned to one of the auto-cohorts when they visit any course discussion topic.

Assigning cohorts manually

To implement the manual assignment strategy, perform the following steps:

1. Click on the blue **View Live** button from within Studio to view the live version of your course.

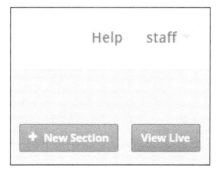

2. Click on **Instructor** to open **Instructor Dashboard**.

3. Click on **Membership** in the **Instructor Dashboard**.

4. Scroll to the **Cohort Management** section at the bottom.

 You might need to click on the **REVERT TO LEGACY DASHBOARD** link to manage cohorts.

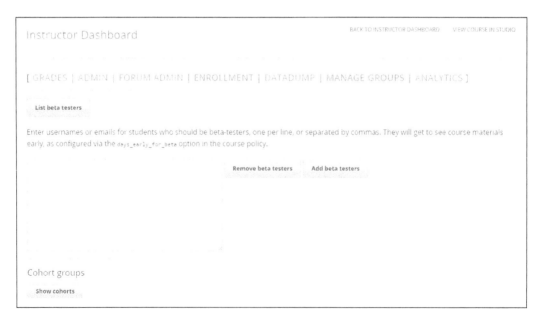

5. Click on the **Show cohorts** button.

6. Add a name for cohort, and click on **Save** below the **Add cohort** button.

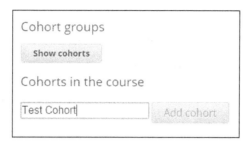

7. View your new cohort name.

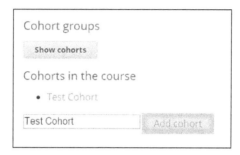

8. Select a desired cohort from the list of those available.

9. Enter the username or e-mail address of a single student.

 You can also enter multiple names or e-mail addresses, separated by commas or on new lines. Alternatively, you can copy data from a CSV file of e-mail addresses and paste it in this field.

10. Click on the **Add Cohort Members** button. Students will then be assigned to the selected manual cohort.

 A message will appear, indicating the number of students who were added to the cohort. The message will also indicate the number of students whose assignment to another cohort was changed by this procedure.

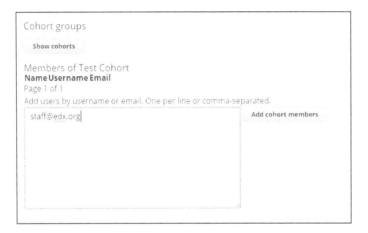

 For a report that includes the cohort assignment for every enrolled student, you should review the student profile information for your course.

Assigning cohorts with a CSV file

Follow these steps to assign students to cohorts using a CSV file:

1. Click on the blue **View Live** button from within Studio to view the live version of your course.

2. Click on **Instructor** to open the **Instructor Dashboard**.

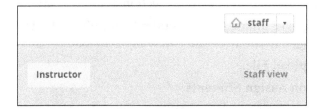

3. Click on **MEMBERSHIP** in the **Instructor Dashboard**.

4. Scroll to the **Cohort Management** section at the bottom.

 You might need to click on the **REVERT TO LEGACY DASHBOARD** link to manage cohorts.

Instructor Dashboard   BACK TO INSTRUCTOR DASHBOARD   VIEW COURSE IN STUDIO

[GRADES | ADMIN | FORUM ADMIN | ENROLLMENT | DATADUMP | MANAGE GROUPS | ANALYTICS]

List beta testers

Enter usernames or emails for students who should be beta-testers, one per line, or separated by commas. They will get to see course materials early, as configured via the days_early_for_beta option in the course policy.

Remove beta testers   Add beta testers

Cohort groups

Show cohorts

5. Click on the **Show cohorts** button.

6. Scroll to the **Cohort Management** section at the bottom.

7. Click on **Browse** under **Assign Students to Cohorts by Uploading a CSV file** to navigate to the .csv file you want to upload.

8. Click on **Upload File**.

9. Then click on **Assign Students**.

10. Verify your upload results on the **Data Download** page.

11. Locate the link to the .csv file with **cohort_results**, and the date and time of your upload in the filename.

 The list of available reports is sorted chronologically under **Reports Available for Download**; the most recently generated files are at the top.

Disabling cohorts

To disable the cohort feature, perform the following steps:

- Follow the instructions for enabling the cohort feature, but set `cohorted: false`. All discussion posts will immediately become visible to all students.

 If you re-enable the cohort feature by setting `cohorted: true`, all visibility settings for posts are reapplied. However, posts created while the cohort feature was disabled remain visible to all users.

Policy Key:

cohort_config

Policy Value:

```
{
    "auto_cohort_groups": [
        "Test Group 1",
        "Test Group 2",
        "Test Group 3"
    ],
    "cohorted": false
}
```

Beta testing

Beta-testing your course is an important process, through which you can assess your progress, test your work, identify gaps and errors, and simulate the student experience. The phases of the beta testing process include the following:

- **Planning**: Define your objectives and determine the schedule for testing.

- **Recruiting**: Determine the number of beta testers you need, estimate how much time you think they will need, and establish a deadline by when feedback needs to be received.

- **Assigning roles**: Define the roles and responsibilities you expect from your beta testers. Likewise, indicate the limits of their involvement to define boundaries.

- **Accessing your course**: Decide whether beta testers can access your entire course immediately, or whether they should be limited to specific sections and subsections.

- **Collecting feedback**: Identify the way for beta testers to deliver feedback. Create the forms, processes, and procedures for them to follow, and identify the tools for them to use.

 Learn how to create a questionnaire to collect feedback by reading the article *How to Make a Questionnaire* at http://www.wikihow. com/Make-a-Questionnaire.

- **Evaluating Feedback**: Establish the process you will be following to evaluate the feedback and actions you will—or won't—take in response.

- **Finishing**: Determine the ways by which you will acknowledge the efforts of your testers. Also determine what you will—and won't—share with them about their efforts.

More about Beta Testers

Beta testers should interact with everything in the course, making sure to:

- Click on all links
- Complete all problems in the course
- Download video transcripts and other files
- Watch all videos

Before adding beta testers, make sure that they have provided you with their e-mail address or the username they are using in your edX installation. Also, have each beta tester register and activate their user account for that e-mail address or username before you get started.

When you are ready to add beta testers, consider the following:

- If the beta test begins before the course's enrollment start date, testers cannot enroll themselves, but you can enroll them prior to the enrollment start date.
- If you add beta testers after the start of the beta test and they are enrolled for the course, they will see your course on their **Current Courses** dashboards.
- If you add beta testers before the test starts or if they are not enrolled, they will not see your course on their dashboards. You can enroll the beta testers for the course; you may want to e-mail them when the test begins.

Adding an individual Beta Tester

To add an individual beta tester, do these steps:

1. View the live version of your course.
2. Click on **Instructor** and then on **Membership**.
3. Navigate to the drop-down list in the **ADMINISTRATION LIST MANAGEMENT** section, and select **Beta Testers** in the drop-down menu under **Select an Administrator Group**.

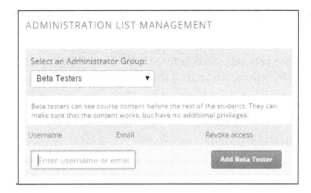

4. Enter an e-mail address or username. Click on the blue **Add Beta Tester** button.

Adding multiple Beta Testers

To add multiple beta testers, perform the following steps:

1. View the live version of your course.

2. Click on **Instructor** and then on **Membership**.

3. Navigate to the **BATCH BETA TESTER ADDITION** section of the page.

4. Enter one or more addresses or usernames, separated by commas or line breaks (that is, by pressing the *Enter* key). You can also copy data from a CSV file of e-mail addresses and paste it here.

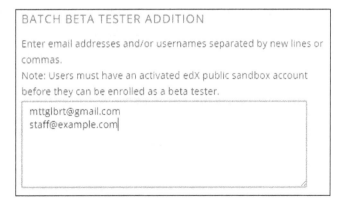

5. Leave **Auto Enroll** selected to enroll beta testers for your course.

 If the beta test starts before the course's Enrollment Start Date, testers can't enroll themselves.

6. Leave **Notify users by email** selected to send an e-mail message to the beta testers.

 An example of the message sent to a beta tester who is not enrolled (or auto-enrolled) in the course is as follows: **You have been invited to be a beta tester for {course name} at {URL}. Visit {link} to join the course and begin the beta test.**

7. Click on **Add Beta Testers**.

Removing Beta Testers

You can remove beta tester cap abilities one user at a time, or you can remove multiple beta testers at once. Here are the steps you need to perform to remove an individual beta tester:

1. Find the user in the list of beta testers.

2. Click on **Revoke Access** to the right of that user's e-mail address.

To remove multiple beta testers, perform these steps:

1. Enter their e-mail addresses in the **BATCH BETA TESTER ADDITION** field.

2. Click on the gray **Remove beta testers** button.

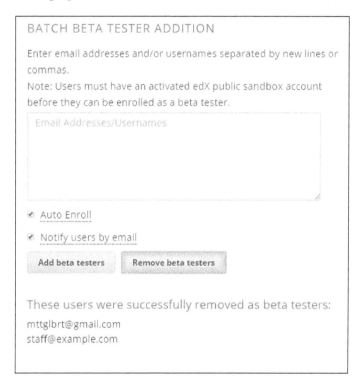

Exporting and importing a course

The ability to export and import your course gives you greater control over your content. You might need to export your course for these reasons:

- To create a backup copy of your course that you can import at a later date if you need to revert to a previous version of the course

- To create a copy of your course that you can later import into another course

- To directly edit the XML in your course

- To save your work

- To share your course content with an instructor teaching another class

When you export your course, Studio compresses all the course files into one file with the `.tar.gz` extension. This file uses a standard GNU zip (`.gzip`) compression algorithm that is commonly used on Unix operating systems to package files, programs, and installers. This file includes:

- Course assets
- Course content (all sections, subsections, and units)
- Course settings
- Course structure
- Individual problems
- Pages

However, the following data will not be exported with your course:

- Certificates
- Course team data
- Discussion data
- User data

 To learn more about `.tar.gz` files read the article *.TAR.GZ File Extension* at `http://fileinfo.com/extension/tar.gz`.

Exporting a course

To export a course, perform the following steps:

1. Log in to Studio and navigate to the course.
2. Select **Export** from the **Tools** menu.

3. Click on the blue **Export Course Content** button.

4. Locate the `.tar.gz` file on your computer when the export completes.

Name	Date modified	Type	Size
edx_demo_course.FTNY50.tar.gz	4/25/2015 10:26 PM	WinZip File	10,733 KB

5. Double-click on the `.tar.gz` file and let your computer select an application to open it.

 You might need to install a compression program, such as WinZip, which you can download at `http://www.winzip.com/prod_down.html`.

Importing a course

The course you import must also be a `.tar.gz` file; edX won't accept any other type. In addition, the file must contain a `course.xml` file in a course data directory and have the same name as the course's data directory; it might also contain other files.

 If your course uses a legacy layout structure, you might not be able to edit the course in Studio, but it should appear correctly on Edge. Make sure that your course is fully editable by embedding all of its components in a unit.

The import process has five stages in all. Consider the following points relative to the steps 1-5:

- During the first two stages, you must stay on the **Course Import** page
- You can leave this page after the unpacking stage has been completed
- edX advises you against making important changes to your course until the import operation completes

To export a course, follow these steps:

1. Select **Import** from the **Tools** menu.

2. Click on the green **Choose a File to Import** button.

3. Locate the file that you want to upload.

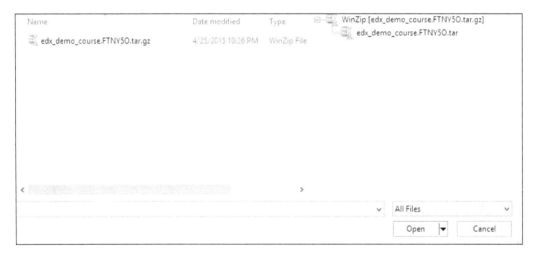

4. Click on **Open**.

5. Then click on the green **Replace my course with the one above** button.

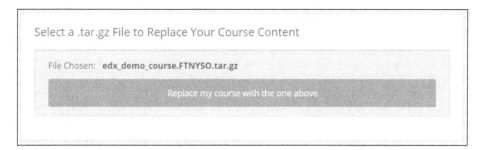

edX resources

Whether you're creating an edX course for your university, or developing a training module for a private organization, there are several online resources available.

Building and running an edX course

EdX maintains an online working reference document titled *Building and Running an edX Course*; this book was developed in part by using this resource. It is updated often but, on occasion, it might not match the functionality you see in your edX course. That said, it is comprehensive and full of details about edX.

You can find the document *Building and Running an edX Course* at `http://edx.readthedocs.org/projects/edx-partner-course-staff/en/latest/index.html`.

Google groups

There are two Google user groups available for free. Moderated by edX employees and full of skilled professionals—just like you—who create edX courses, both groups are exceptional virtual communities of practice.

To join either group, simply click on the following links, sign in to your Google account, and join the group:

- **edx-code Google group** (`https://groups.google.com/forum/#!forum/edx-code`): For discussions that span multiple edX projects or are about projects that don't have a dedicated mailing list

- **XBlock Google group** (`https://groups.google.com/forum/#!forum/edx-xblock`): For discussions on XBlock, edX's courseware component architecture

If you don't have a Google account yet, you can create it for free at `https://accounts.google.com/signup`.

GitHub

GitHub is a Web-based, open source repository where people can share versions of code for open source software projects. Currently, it has five pages of code for all the various aspects of edX. You can access all of them from `https://github.com/edx`.

Launching your course

As you approach the start date of the course, follow this checklist to ensure that your course, staff, students, and — most importantly — you are ready to roll:

1. Verify the course settings:
   - Check the course's start date and time in Studio
   - Review the grading policy and set a grace period for homework assignment due dates
   - Confirm that any optional features that you want your course to include, such as implementing student cohorts, are enabled and configured

2. Review the first week's content:
   - Verify that all the required units are present and published
   - Check all the assignments for completeness and verify their due dates
   - Verify that the videos, transcripts, and download links are in place and working
   - Review the feedback from the course team and beta testers to be sure that the content has been thoroughly reviewed and tested

3. Welcome the students:
   - Prepare and send a welcome e-mail to all enrolled students two months before the course start date.
   - Compose a welcome message and add it to the **Course Info** page.
   - Verify that the syllabus and other references are available on the **Course Handouts** page.

- º Prepare and send a welcome e-mail to the currently enrolled students one month before the course start date.
- º Prepare and send a welcome e-mail message to the currently enrolled students one week before the course start date.
- º Add an `Introduce Yourself` post to a discussion topic. Depending on the size of your class, you should consider distributing student responses across multiple threads. You can start different threads for introductions, based on geographical locations, for example.
- º On the start date of the course, prepare and send a launch e-mail to all enrolled students.

4. Prepare the staff:

- º Define the communication methods for all the course contributors, including the staff, instructors, and the discussion team. As an example, set up a course-specific e-mail address.
- º Verify that all the contributors know how to record their work, report issues, and collaborate on tasks.
- º Verify that the instructors and course staff selected for your course have the correct role assignments in the LMS.
- º Verify that the discussion admins, discussion moderators, and community TAs have registered and activated their user accounts, have enrolled in the course, and have been assigned their roles in the **Instructor Dashboard**.
- º Define the methods of managing discussions and guidance for discussion moderators, and distribute your policies and procedures to the discussion team.

Summary

In this chapter, we discussed the administrative functions you will need to manage, along with the best practices and online resources you can use to make your job easier.

We also reviewed how to establish a grading policy, control content visibility, include student cohorts, tackle beta testing, export and import your course, make the most of edX resources, and finally launch your course.

Next, in *Chapter 7, Facilitating Your Course*, we will go to cover factors related to facilitating your course. The topics to be covered include how to select your course staff, invite students to enroll, direct your discussions, manage your messaging, create your course Wiki, review course data, supervise student data, manage the grade book, and issue certificates of completion.

7
Facilitating Your Course

According to a popular American idiom, "home is where the heart is." The idea is that "home" is not a physical place, but a state of mind that you experience whenever you are with your loved ones—or simply wherever you want to be.

Likewise, in January 2015, the *Harvard Business Review* published a report that researched the impact of telecommuting versus working in a typical office. The study found that employees working at home registered an increase in performance by 13 percent while the turnover of the same group decreased by 50 percent.

There was one drawback: half of the employees working at home chose to return to the office citing loneliness as their concern. It was the intrinsically driven employees who weren't distracted by things at home. And so, while working from home has benefits, it also has drawbacks.

Students in your edX course will likely be participating from wherever home is for them. That's the beauty—and the challenge—of edX, just as it is for any online course. Hopefully, your students will be comfortable in their chosen homes, but there is the risk that they will get distracted and succumb to feelings of loneliness.

Knowing this, you will need to set a positive tone when you facilitate your course. While it is each student's responsibility to complete the assignments of your course, you will need to facilitate their overall learning experience. That's where this chapter comes in. Offering the insight you need to facilitate your course in this chapter, we will review how to:

- Assign your staff roles
- Invite students to enroll
- Direct your discussions
- Manage your messaging
- Create your course wiki

- Review the course data
- Supervise the student data
- Oversee the answer data
- Manage the gradebook
- Issue completion certificates

Staff roles

Members of your course team can be assigned to two possible roles: course staff and instructor.

Course staff

The basic responsibility of the course staff is to:

- Access student grades
- Enroll and unenroll students
- Reset student attempts to answer a question
- Review/see course HTML errors
- Send e-mails to participants/students
- View the course before the start date

Instructor

The basic responsibility of the Instructor is to:

- Add and remove beta testers
- Add and remove course staff
- Add and remove Discussion Admins, Discussion Moderators, and Discussion Community Teaching Assistants
- Add and remove other instructors
- Perform all the functions of the course staff

You can designate these roles in the live course or in Studio. Likewise, the individuals you assign these roles to can access your course in either environment. To add course team members, perform these steps:

1. Ensure that you have Admin access.

2. Avoid the two **Error adding user** errors shown in the following screenshot by first verifying that the new team member has already:

    ° Registered a user account for the e-mail address or username they intend to use

    ° Activated their account with that e-mail address or username

    ° Enrolled for your course

3. Select **Course Team** from the **Settings** menu:

4. Click on the green **New Team Member** button:

5. Enter the new user's e-mail address and click on the blue **ADD USER** button:

6. Add a team member in an alternate way by clicking on the green **+ Add a New Team Member** button while viewing the list of current course team members, as shown in the following screenshot:

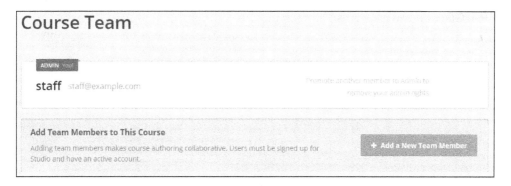

7. Click on the blue **Add Admin Access** button to add administrative privileges to your newly added course staff member, as shown in the following screenshot:

8. Click on the gray **Remove Admin Access** button for any course team member to remove their administrative privileges, as follows:

9. Click on the gray trash can icon to the right of the blue **Add Admin Access** button to remove a member from the course team, as shown in this screenshot:

10. Manage the course staff alternatively in the **ADMINISTRATION LIST MANAGEMENT** area of the **Membership** section of your **Instructor Dashboard**.

 To add a new course team member, enter their username or e-mail address and click on the blue **Add Staff** button. To remove a member from the course team, click on the **Revoke Access** link next to their username or e-mail address. These can be seen in the following screenshot:

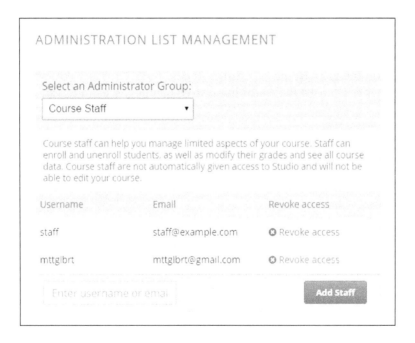

Student enrolment

You can manually enroll students for a course, see how many students are enrolled, and – if needed – unenroll students using the **Instructor Dashboard**. Students can enroll themselves as well during that course's enrollment period.

For a course on edx.org, enrollment is publicly available for anyone with an edX account. For other courses, such as those on edge.edx.org, students can enroll themselves using the course URL you provide (it is not available to the general public); you can also directly enroll students.

Before a student can enroll in a course, they must do the following:

1. **Register a user account**: This requires a valid e-mail address on edx.org, edge.edx.org, or your implementation of the edX platform. Each platform requires a separate user account, but can use the same e-mail address.

2. **Activate the account**: Students must follow instructions e-mailed to them.

If the course's **Enrollment End Date** has not passed, students with registered and activated accounts can enroll themselves in edx.org courses or other courses if they know the URL.

Course authors and instructors can enroll students in a course either before or after the students register their accounts with their e-mail addresses. Course staff members must have registered and activated user accounts and be enrolled in the course.

When you enroll people in a course you have two choices, as discussed in the following sections:

Auto Enroll

*   With **Auto Enroll**, the students you enroll don't need to complete a course enrollment step.

*   E-mail addresses you enter that correspond to a registered user account are immediately enrolled. Your course will then be displayed in those students' **Current Courses** dashboards.

*   E-mail addresses that don't match a registered account are enrolled at the moment when that user account is registered and activated.

*   If you don't select **Auto Enroll**, the students you enroll must then locate your course and enroll themselves in it. They will see your course in their **Current Courses** dashboards once they have done so.

Notify students by e-mail

- When this option is selected, an e-mail is automatically sent to each e-mail address you supply.

- The message includes the name of the course and, for students who are not already enrolled in it, a reminder to use the same e-mail address to enroll.

- An example of the e-mail message is as follows. Note that the student already had a registered and activated edx.org account, and both **Auto Enroll** and **Notify students by email** were selected.

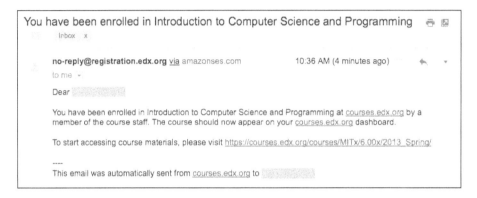

To enroll students or staff members, perform the following steps:

1. Enter the live version of your course by clicking on the **View Live** button:

2. Click on **Instructor** and then on **Membership**.

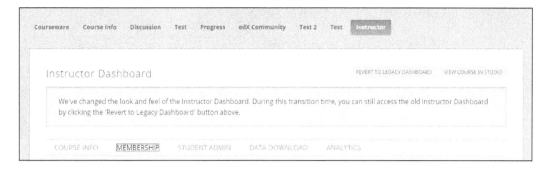

3. Enter the username or e-mail address of the students you wish to enroll in the **BATCH ENROLLMENT** section of the page, separated by commas or new lines.

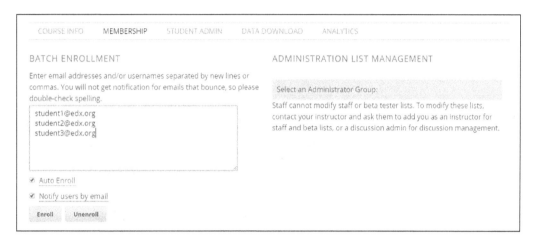

4. Copy-and-paste data from a CSV file of e-mail addresses to alternately enroll students, but this feature is better suited for courses with smaller enrollments.

5. Leave the **Auto Enroll** box checked to streamline the enrollment process.

6. Leave the **Notify users by email** box checked to have the system send students an enrollment e-mail.

7. Click on the gray **Enroll** button.

Once you've enrolled students in your course, you can access the total number of people enrolled in it with the enrollment count. This feature displays the number of students and course team staff who are currently enrolled; it is not a historical count of everyone who was ever enrolled in the course.

To view the enrollment count, perform these steps:

1. Enter the live version of your course.

2. Click on **Instructor** and then on **Course Info**.

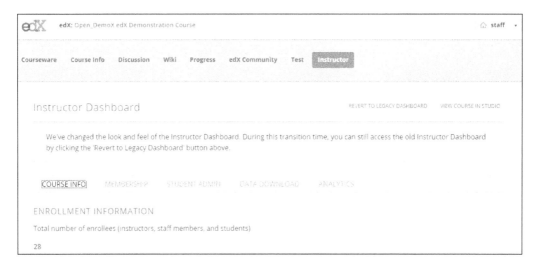

At any time of their choice, students can unenroll from your course, and course staff can, likewise, unenroll students when necessary. To prevent students from re-enrolling, you should close course enrollment by using Studio to set **Enrollment End Date** for the course to a date in the past.

 Unenrolling a student does not delete the data about that student. Their data remains in the database, and is reinstated if the student enrolls again.

To unenroll a student, follow these steps:

1. Enter the live version of your course.

2. Click on **Membership**.

3. Enter a username or an e-mail address—or multiple names or addresses separated by commas or new lines—you wish to unenroll in the **BATCH ENROLLMENT** section.

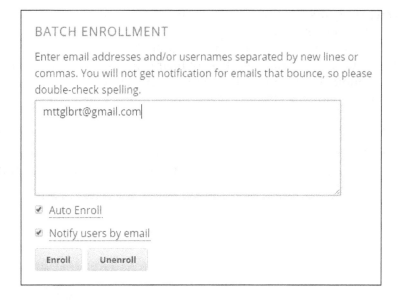

4. Leave the **Auto Enroll** box checked to streamline the enrollment process.

5. Leave the **Notify users by email** box checked to have the system send students an enrollment e-mail.

6. Click on the gray **Unenroll** button. The course will no longer appear in the student's **Current Courses** dashboard, and unenrolled students can no longer contribute to discussions or the wiki or access the courseware.

Course discussions

Course discussions encourage interaction among students and the course staff. You can set up different topics to encourage engagement and create a community. Discussions are also good sources of feedback. A discussion offers three hierarchical levels of interaction:

- **Post**: This opens a new subject. It is often posed as questions, either to start a conversation or to bring up an issue that requires action. When you add a post, you categorize it as a question or a discussion.

- **Response**: This is a reply made directly to a post to offer an insight or a solution in a way that continues the conversation.

- **Comment**: This is often a clarification made to a specific response rather than to the post as a whole.

When you create a course, a discussion topic named "General" is available by default; you can add more course-wide discussions. In courses with cohorts enabled, all course-wide discussion topics you add are unified. All the posts can be read and responded to by every student, regardless of their cohort assignment. You can also configure these topics to be divided by cohort. To create a course-wide discussion topic, perform the following steps:

1. Open your course in Studio.

2. Select **Settings** and then **Advanced Settings**.

3. Scroll down to the **Discussion Topic Mapping** policy key. By default, its value is as shown in the following screenshot:

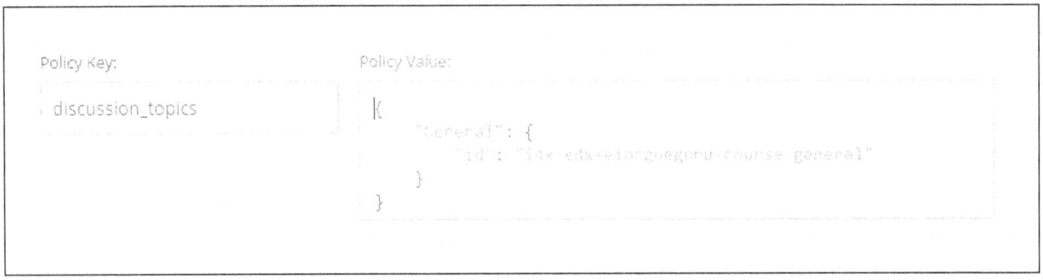

4. Copy the three lines provided for the "General" topic and paste them above the closing brace, }.

5. Replace the second "General" with the quoted name of your new topic ("Class Connect" in this example).

6. Change the value for the second "id" to a unique identifier; for example, append a reference to the name of the topic.

7. Add a comma after the first closing brace, like this: },.

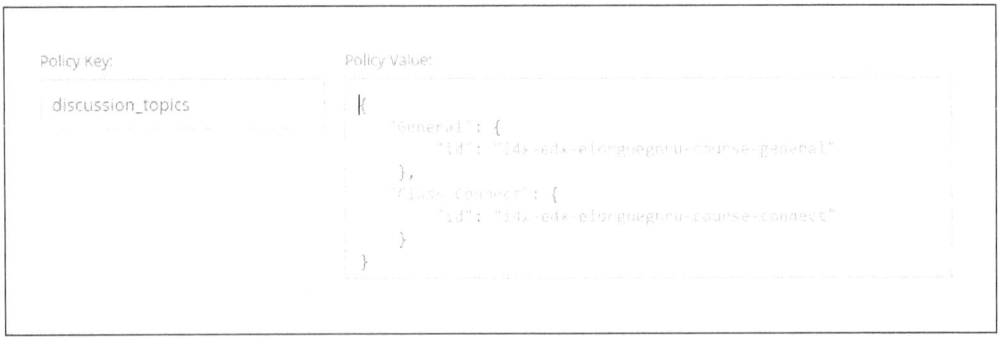

8. Click on the yellow **Save Changes** button.

[Studio resequences and reformats your entry.]

9. Scroll back to the **Discussion Topic Mapping** field to verify that the drop-down discussion list now includes the topic you added.

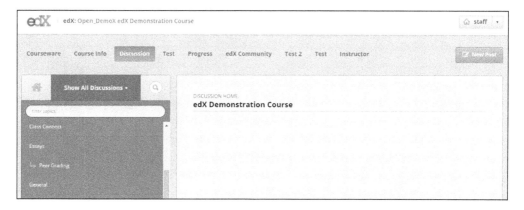

You can identify a team of people to help you facilitate discussions in your course. The roles to which you can assign students or staff members include the following:

- **Discussion Moderators**: These can edit and delete messages at any level, review messages flagged for misuse, close and reopen posts, pin posts, and endorse responses. This role is often given to course staff members.

- **Discussion Community TAs**: These have the same options for working with discussions as moderators. This role is often given to students.

- **Discussion Admins**: These have the same options for working with discussions as moderators. This role can be reserved for course team members who have the instructor role only. Discussion admins can then moderate discussions and give other users these discussion management roles whenever necessary.

Before you can assign these roles, you will need the e-mail addresses or usernames of the selected course team members or students. For a course team member, click on **Membership** and **Course Staff** or **Instructor** from the drop-down list on the **Instructor Dashboard**.

For an enrolled student, perform these steps:

1. Click on **Data Download**.
2. Download the profile information as a CSV file.

To assign a discussion administration role, you must be either the course author or an instructor. Once that has been confirmed, follow these steps:

1. Enter the live version of the course.

2. Click on **Instructor** and then on **Membership**.

3. Use the drop-down menu to select an **Administrator Group** from the list.

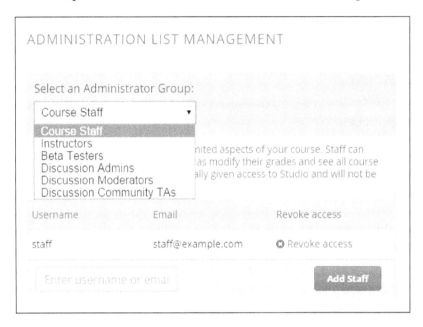

4. Enter an e-mail address or username, and click on the blue **Add Staff** button for the role type under the list of users who currently have that role.

5. Remove an assigned role by viewing the list of users and clicking on **Revoke access**.

As you manage your course's discussions, consider these best practices:

- **Close a post**: Respond to a redundant post by pasting a link to the post you prefer students to contribute to, thereby preventing further interaction by closing the post. Select the **More** icon and then **Close** to close it.

- **Develop a positive culture**: Cultivate positive qualities in your discussions and interactions to make the student's time productive.

- **Endorse a response**: Endorsing a response adds value to the discussion. Click on the **Check Mark** icon for the response.

- **Mark a question as answered**: Use the same procedure to mark a response as the correct answer to a question as we used when endorsing contributions to a discussion: click on the **Check Mark** icon for the response.

- **Moderate discussions**: Monitor discussions and keep them productive. You can also collect information, such as areas of particular confusion or interest, and relay it to the course staff.

- **Pin a post**: Pinning a post makes it appear at the top of the list of posts; then it is more likely that students will see and respond to it. Write your own post and pin it, or pin a post by any author. Select the **More** icon and then select **Pin**.

- **Provide guidelines for students**: Develop best practices for participation in discussions, and share them with students as a course handout file or on a defined page in your course. These guidelines can define your expectations and optionally introduce features of edX discussions.

- **Seed discussions**: Help students get the most out of course discussions by seeding discussion topics (adding posts before your course starts).

If you need to edit a post, perform these steps:

1. Log in to the site and select the course on your **Current Courses** dashboard.

2. Open the **Discussion** page and view the post with the content that requires editing.

3. Select a single topic from the drop-down list of discussion topics, apply a filter, or search to locate the post.

4. Click on the **More** icon and then the **Edit** icon.

5. Remove the problematic portion of the message, or replace it with standard text, such as [REMOVED BY MODERATOR].

6. Communicate the reason for your change. For example, Posting a solution violates the honor code.

If you would like to delete a post, perform the following steps:

1. Log in to the site and then select the course on your **Current Courses** dashboard.

2. Open the **Discussion** page and view the post with the content requiring deletion.

3. Select a single topic from the drop-down list of discussion topics, apply a filter, or search to locate the post.

4. Click on the **More** icon and then on **Delete** to delete the post.

5. Click on **OK** to confirm the deletion.

If you receive a report of misuse, you can respond to it, as follows:

1. View the live version of your course.

2. Click on **Discussion** at the top of the page.

3. Use the filter drop-down list (set to **Show all by default**) to select **Flagged** in the list of posts on the left side of the page.

4. Review the listed posts; the reported contribution includes a reported identifier.

5. Edit or delete the post, response, or comment.

Alternately, you can go for the following steps:

1. Remove the flag.

2. Click on the **More** icon.

3. Click on **Unreport**.

> If a student continues to misuse the discussions, you can unenroll them from the course. If the enrollment period for the course is over, that student can't re-enroll. You can also close the discussions so that students cannot add messages. Course discussions can be closed temporarily or permanently.

To define when discussions are closed to new contributions and when they reopen, follow these steps:

1. Open your course in Studio.

2. Select **Settings** and then **Advanced Settings**.

3. Scroll down to the **Discussion Blackout Dates** policy key.

4. Place your cursor between the square brackets in the field for the value.

5. Use the required date format specification to enter the start and end dates for each time period during which you want discussions to be closed.

6. Click on **Save Changes**.

Studio reformats your entry to add linefeeds and indentation, like this:

```
Policy Key:                     Policy Value:

discussion_blackouts            [
                                    [
                                        "2015-01-01T08:00",
                                        "2015-01-10T08:00"
                                    ],
                                    [
                                        "2015-02-01T08:00",
                                        "2015-02-10T08:00"
                                    ],
                                    [
                                        "2015-03-01T08:00",
                                        "2015-03-10T08:00"
                                    ]
                                ]
```

Course Wiki

The course Wiki provides a platform where your course staff and students can access, share, and collaboratively edit information for and about your course. You can influence the way your wiki is used by seeding it with specific content, explaining how you want it to be used and providing clear instructions and guidelines for its use. Consider using your course wiki for these purposes:

- Collect suggestions for future runs of the course
- Give shared access to student-created resources, perhaps as a part of a collaborative exercise
- Provide answers to course FAQs and collecting new FAQs
- Publish errata for the course
- Share editable course information, such as download and installation instructions for the software required for the course

If you don't want to use a wiki in your course, you can hide the **Wiki** tab at the top of the course by following these steps:

1. Open your course in Studio.

2. Select **Content** and then click on **Pages**.

3. Click on the eye icon in the **Wiki** row. The **Wiki** tab is hidden when this icon has a slash through it. You can show the **Wiki** tab again by clicking on this icon:

When you hide the wiki in your course, existing articles still remain in the edX-wide wiki, but the **Wiki** tab is removed from your course pages.

You can also control access to the wiki by:

- Restricting access to the wiki as a whole
- Changing the read-write permission settings of articles within the wiki
- Locking articles

To change access to the course wiki, follow these steps:

1. Open your course in Studio.
2. Select **Settings** and then **Advanced Settings**.

3. Scroll down to the **allow_public_wiki_access** policy key.

 When set to **False** (by default), only course team members and enrolled students can see the Wiki. Change the value to **True**, and any registered edX user can access the Wiki, even if they are not enrolled in your course. Public users will have to explicitly navigate to your wiki via the edX-wide wiki structure, or via a link.

If you want to prevent certain groups of users from adding or editing articles on your Wiki (an example would be preventing students from creating top-level articles), you need to modify the read-write permissions for articles, which is done as follows:

1. Enter the live version of your course.

2. Click on **Wiki**.

3. Navigate to the article for which you want to change the permissions.

4. Click on **Settings**.

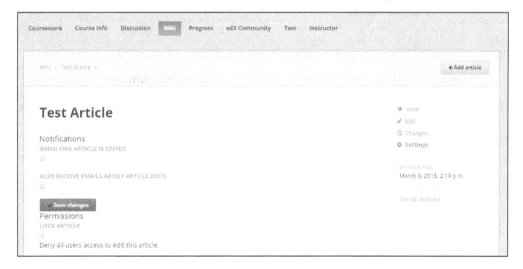

5. Select the suitable checkboxes from **GROUP READ ACCESS, GROUP WRITE ACCESS, OTHERS READ ACCESS, OTHERS WRITE ACCESS,** and **INHERIT PERMISSIONS**.

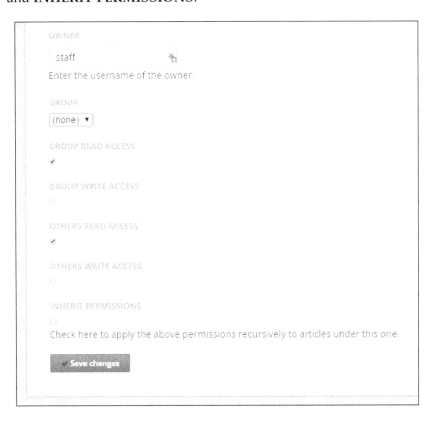

6. Click on the blue **Save changes** button for the permissions section.

When you want to add an article to the Wiki, be mindful of the level you are viewing so that you add your new article to the correct level in the course wiki. To move down a level in your Wiki, click on the **See all children** link. To move up, click on the appropriate level in the wiki breadcrumb trail links at the top of the page.

Follow these steps to add a wiki article at your current level in the Wiki:

1. Navigate to the level where you want to add a new article.
2. Click on the gray **Add article** button near the top-right corner of the page.

3. Add a title for the page and a few keywords to create a slug that provides a more specific location identifier for your article on the new article page.
4. Add content to the article. You can enter plain text and use markdown syntax to add formatting.

 For help with markdown syntax, click on the link to the cheat sheet in the top-right corner of the **Contents** field.

5. Click on **Create article** when you're done with entering content.

Follow these steps to add a child article to your current article:

1. Click on **Wiki** in your live course.
2. Navigate to the level where you want to add the new child article.
3. Click on the **See all children** link.

4. Then click on the **Add article** button under the Wiki title.

5. Add a title for the page and a few keywords to create a slug that provides a more specific location identifier for your article.

6. Add content to the article. You can enter plain text and use markdown syntax to add formatting.

7. Click on the blue **+ Create article** button when you're done.

If you have permissions to edit an article, you will see an **Edit** button and an icon to the right of the article content. Follow these steps to make changes to a Wiki article:

1. Click on **Wiki** in your live course.

2. Navigate to the article you want to edit.

3. Click on the **Edit** link and view the various available options.

4. Make your desired changes.
5. Enter a short description of the changes you made in the **Summary** field in the bottom-left corner (below the **Contents** field).

> This description appears in the **Changes** list. It helps other users understand what changes you've made to the article.

6. Click on the gray **Preview** button to see how your wiki article will look when live.
7. Click on the blue **Save changes** button when you are done with making edits.
8. Click on the red **Delete article** button if you wish to delete the article.

The Wiki includes a history of all the changes made to each article. You can:

- View each past version
- Roll back to a selected earlier version of the article
- Merge the current version of the article with a selected earlier version

To view a list of previous versions of a wiki article, follow these steps:

1. Click on **Wiki** in your live course.
2. Navigate to the wiki article for which you want to see the change history.

3. Click on **Changes**.

 Here, you'll see that all previously saved versions of the current article are listed, with the most recent at the top.

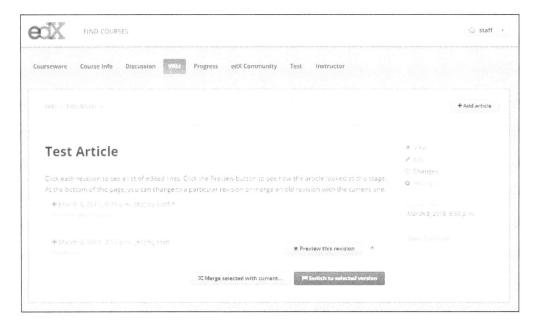

To view a previous version of a wiki article, perform the following steps:

1. Select the revision of the article that you want to view on the **Changes** page.

2. Click on **Preview this revision** to see the article as it appeared previously.

To replace a current version with a previous version, follow these steps:

1. Select the revision of the article to which you want to roll back.

2. Click on the blue **Switch to selected version** button.

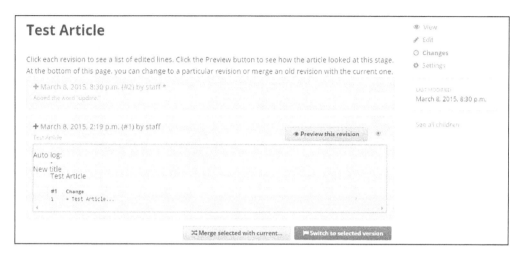

Perform these steps to combine a current version with a previous version:

1. Select the revision of the article you want to merge with the current article.

2. Click on the gray **Merge selected with current...** button to combine the two versions.

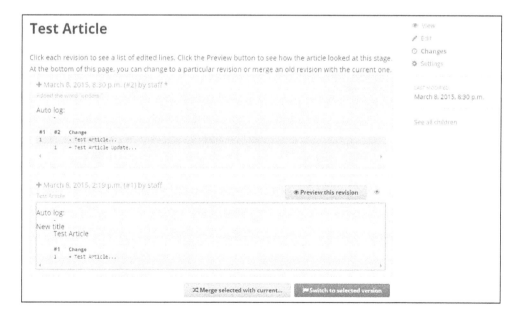

Locking a wiki article prevents further changes from being made to it. Follow these steps to lock a wiki article, either after you've created it or after you've made specific edits:

1. View the live version of your course.

2. Click on **Wiki**.

3. Navigate to the article you want to lock, and then click on **Settings**.

4. Select the **LOCK ARTICLE** checkbox in the **Permissions** section of the **Settings** page.

5. Click on the blue **Save changes** button.

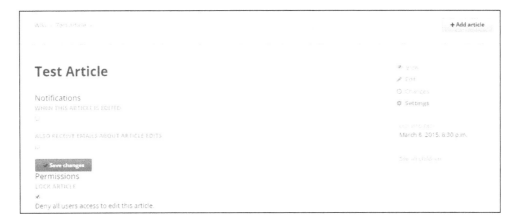

If you have the required permissions, you can follow these steps to delete an article:

1. View the live version of your course.

2. Click on **Wiki**.

3. Navigate to the article you want to delete, and then click on **Edit**.

4. Click on the red **Delete article** button.

5. On the deletion confirmation page, select **YES, I AM SURE**.

 Optionally, you can select the **Purge** checkbox.

6. Click on **Delete article** to confirm the deletion.

 Articles that have been deleted but not purged can be restored. A link to the article is visible at the level where it was created. To restore a deleted article, click on the link to the article and then click on **Restore**.

A filter field for searching throughout the Wiki to find articles is available, but it works only if the Wiki contains multiple articles. If this is the case, use these steps to search for a Wiki article:

1. Enter your live course and click on **Wiki**.

2. Navigate to the top level of the Wiki by clicking on the **Wiki** link when it turns red.

3. Click on the **See all children** link in the bottom-right corner of the page.

4. Enter a text string in the **Filter** field to find all articles with that string.

5. Press the *Enter* key on your keyboard and click on the appropriate result.

Messages to students

Communication with your students is crucial in any online educational environment, but it is especially important in a MOOC, where students can more easily feel overwhelmed or lost in the crowd. For courses offered on edx.org, the system provides you with a way to send bulk e-mails to course participants from the **Instructor Dashboard**.

The messages you send via edX can use HTML styling, and can include links to videos, social media pages for the course, and any other relevant material. Anyone assigned as course staff or instructor can send bulk e-mails to communicate with course participants, before, during, and after the course.

When sending a message, you have to select its recipients by identifying them as belonging to one of these predefined groups:

- **Myself**: Select this to send a message to yourself. This is useful for testing messages before you send them to the class.

- **Staff and Instructors**: Choose this when you want to send a message to other members of the administrative team.

- **All**: Selecting this will send a message to all currently enrolled students, staff, and instructors.

When you send an e-mail to **All**, it will be delivered to all enrolled students, except:

- Students who have not replied to the account activation e-mail
- Students who opted out of receiving e-mails via the **Email Settings** link

Before you use the bulk e-mail feature, remember that messages can't be canceled after they are sent. If you plan to send a message to all course participants, be sure to review each draft carefully, sending the message to yourself for testing.

Writing and saving your e-mails in Microsoft Word (or another word-processing program of your choice) might be an effective way to manage your messages, ensure their accuracy, and archive them for future use. You can copy and paste the message content into edX from the most current document.

 Include revision dates or version numbers with the filename of each new version of your e-mails and file older versions in an electronic archive folder. Consider using a YYYYMMDD date format to facilitate easy sorting and file management.

To send a message, follow these steps:

1. View the live version of your course.
2. Click on **Instructor** and then on **Email**.
3. Select who you want to send the message to from the **Send to** drop-down list: **Myself**, **Staff and Instructors**, or **All** (you, staff, instructors, and students).
4. Enter a **Subject** for the message.
5. Enter the text for the message.
6. Include an image in your message by first adding the file using the **Files & Uploads** page in **Studio**, then clicking on the **Insert/edit image** icon.
7. Add HTML styling, including text formatting and links. The e-mail message editor offers the same formatting options as the HTML editor in Studio.
8. Click on **Send Email**.

You can perform other tasks on the **Instructor Dashboard**, or navigate to other pages while you wait for your message to be sent.

After you've sent a message, a bulk e-mail task is queued for processing. Multiple courses use the same queue to complete these tasks, so it can take some time for your message to be sent to all its recipients.

If your course is a MOOC, consider limiting the number of messages that you send to all course participants to no more than one per week.

After you click on **Send Email** for a message, the server begins to process a bulk e-mail. The server assigns a series of different workflow states to the task. These are explained in the order in which they occur:

1. **Queuing**: The bulk e-mail task is queued for background processing.

2. **Pending**: The bulk e-mail task is queued and is waiting to run.

3. **Started**: Background processing creates e-mailing subtasks.

4. **Progress**: The e-mailing subtasks are in progress.

5. **Success**: All e-mailing subtasks are complete. The bulk e-mail task can be in this state even if some or all of its e-mailing subtasks have failed.

6. **Failure**: An error occurs, and the task processing is unsuccessful.

You can review the subject line, the username of the person who sent it, the date and time when it was sent, the recipients, and the message text for any message sent. To do so, follow these steps:

1. View the live version of your course.

2. Click on **Instructor** and then on **Email**.

3. Click on **Sent Email History** in the **Email Task History** section of the page.

4. Click on the subject of a message to review the additional information for the message.

Optionally, you can use the message as the basis for a new message: click on **Copy Email to Editor**. The dialog box closes, and you can edit the text, links, and formatting that was duplicated in the **Subject** and **Message** fields. Be sure to review and test it before you send it to all course participants.

From a best-practice perspective, you should consider writing templates for e-mails you will send for course milestones; consider the following:

- **Pre-Launch reminder**: Raise awareness of the course's start date, publicize the course, and generate excitement.

- **Launch day welcome**: Welcome students and give them specific actions to accomplish.

- **Reminder to register for verified certificate**: Remind students that the last day to register for a verified certificate is approaching.

- **Weekly highlights**: Summarize the content covered each week, and remind students about upcoming assessments or milestones in the course. Optionally, to encourage participation in the discussion forums, you might also highlight interesting or important discussions, and give links to the discussion topics.

- **Mid-course encouragement**: Send messages to promote your community, remind students of upcoming due dates, and address any recurring issues.

- **Mid-course event**: Before an exam or a significant course event, messages can provide practical information, communicate expectations regarding conduct, and also encourage students to continue working towards course completion.

- **Technical issue**: A message can alert students to the problem and reassure them that the issue is either resolved or being addressed. It can also provide information about any changes made to the course as a result.

- **Course farewell and certificates**: Direct students to a course survey, answer questions about certificates, and provide information about future access to course materials.

- **New course run announcement**: Highlight the key aspects of the course, or reveal new features or content that may have been added. Emphasize the value of the course, get people thinking and talking about their experiences, build excitement, and encourage re-enrollment.

Course data

After you've created a course, you can access information about it from the **Instructor Dashboard**, including these:

- Identifying information on the course

- Whether the course has started or ended

- The defined grade cutoff for passing or failing

Additional information about the course and its students can be found on other pages in the **Instructor Dashboard**. You can also acquire information from edX Insights, which you can also access from the **Instructor Dashboard**: simply click on the link in the banner at the top of each page. To view course data, follow these steps:

1. View the live version of your course.

2. Click on **Instructor** then on **Course Info** (if necessary).

 The **BASIC COURSE INFORMATION** section of the page that opens lists information about the course.

Instructor Dashboard   REVERT TO LEGACY DASHBOARD   VIEW COURSE IN STUDIO

We've changed the look and feel of the Instructor Dashboard. During this transition time, you can still access the old Instructor Dashboard by clicking the 'Revert to Legacy Dashboard' button above.

COURSE INFO   MEMBERSHIP   STUDENT ADMIN   DATA DOWNLOAD   ANALYTICS

ENROLLMENT INFORMATION

Total number of enrollees (instructors, staff members, and students)

27

BASIC COURSE INFORMATION

- Organization: **edX**
- Course Number: **Open_DemoX**
- Course Name: **edx_demo_course**
- Course Display Name: **edX Demonstration Course**
- Has the course started? **Yes**
- Has the course ended? **No**
- Grade Cutoffs: **D: 0.59, B: 0.7, C: 0.65, A: 0.8**

PENDING INSTRUCTOR TASKS

The status for any active tasks appears in a table below.

The course data that is displayed on the **Instructor Dashboard** is defined in Studio, or derived from data that you define in Studio. It includes the following pieces of information:

- **Organization**: This is specified in Studio when you create the course. It is a part of the course URL and cannot be changed.

- **Course Number**: This is specified in Studio when you create the course. It is a part of the course URL and cannot be changed.

- **Course Name**: This is specified in Studio when you create the course. It is labeled course run. It is a part of the course URL and cannot be changed.

- **Course Display Name**: This is specified in Studio when you create the course. This field is labeled **Course Name**. The value for the **Course Display Name** policy key defines the course name that appears in the LMS only. This name can be changed (not recommended for a live course)—from the **Settings** menu, select **Advanced Settings**.

- **Has the course started?**: Derived from **Course Start Date** and the current date, this date can be changed in Studio (not recommended for a live course) by selecting **Settings** and then **Schedule & Details**.

- **Has the course ended?**: Derived from **Course End Date** and the current date, this date can be changed in Studio (not recommended for a live course) by selecting **Settings** and then **Schedule & Details**.

- **Grade Cutoffs**: This is specified in Studio when you define the cutoff for a failing grade. Students who earn exactly the cutoff value pass the course. Grading can be changed in Studio (not recommended for a live course) by selecting **Settings** and then **Grading**.

Student data

Data about the students enrolled in your course is available for review. You can download this data in a comma-separated values file (CSV); or, for courses with fewer than 200 students, you can view data for enrolled students on the **Instructor Dashboard**.

When students register with edX, they select a public username and supply information about themselves. Most of this information is optional, so not all students who are enrolled in your course provide it.

Student data reflects only current enrollments; students can enroll in your course during the defined enrollment period, and they can unenroll from a course at any time. Students can also change their e-mail addresses and names at any time. Therefore, you should download student data periodically to gain insights into the student population over time.

To download student data, perform these steps:

1. View the live version of your course.

2. Click on **Instructor** and then on **Data Download**.

3. Click on the gray **Download profile information as a CSV** button to download data as a CSV file.

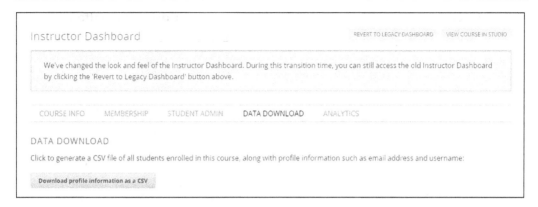

 A status message indicates that report generation is in progress. This process can take some time to complete, but you are able to navigate away from this page and do any other work while it runs.

4. Reload the page in your browser, and scroll down to the **PENDING INSTRUCTION TASKS** section to track the progress of the report process.

5. Open or save a student data report by clicking on the {course_id}_ student_profile_info_{date}.csv filename at the bottom of the page.

 All student-supplied data is included in this file without truncation.

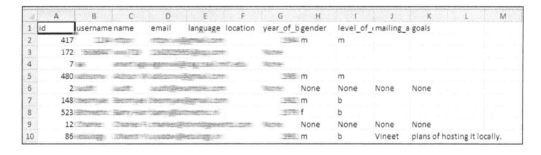

To view student data (for courses with an enrollment of fewer than 200), follow these steps:

1. View the live version of your course.

2. Click on **Instructor** and then on **Data Download**.

3. Click on the gray **List enrolled students' profile information** button.

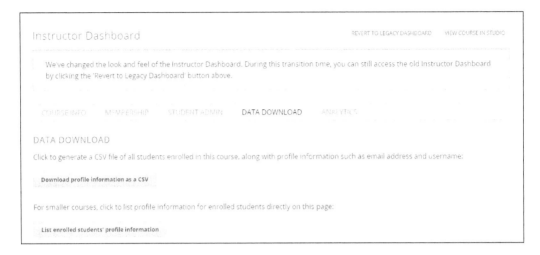

 A table of the student data shows up, with one row for each enrolled student. Longer values, such as student goals, are truncated. For courses that have the cohorts feature enabled, this report also includes a Cohort column with each student's assigned cohort group.

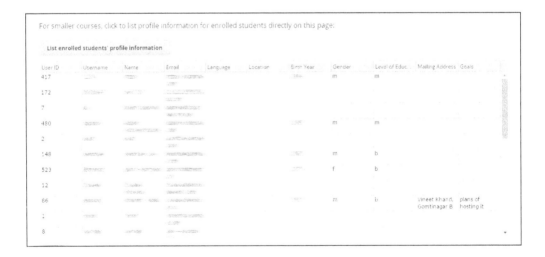

Some of the tools that you can use with the edX platform (for example, external graders and surveys) work with anonymized student data. If you need to deanonymize previously anonymized data, you can download a CSV file of assigned user IDs and anonymized user IDs, as follows:

1. View the live version of your course.

2. Click on **Instructor** and then on **Data Download**.

3. Click on **Get Student Anonymized IDs CSV**.

4. Open or save the {course-id}-anon-id.csv file.

 This file contains the user ID assigned to each student at registration and its edX-wide anonymized user ID. Values are included for every student who ever enrolled for your course.

5. Use this file with the {course_id}_student_profile_info_{date}.csv file of student data or the {course_id}_grade_report_{date}.csv file of grades to research and deanonymize student data.

You should monitor student activity by reviewing the number of students who interact with your course each week.

 To be considered active, students must visit pages, play videos, add to discussions, submit answers to problems, or complete other course activities. The active student count is updated weekly.

To display the number of active students in your course, perform the following steps:

1. View the live version of your course.

2. Click on **Instructor** and then on **Analytics**.

 The count of active students appears at the top of the page.

Answer data

If the need arises, you can review the answer submitted by a selected student for a specific problem, download a course-wide report of answer data, or review a histogram of student answers for a selected problem.

To review a response submitted by a student, follow these steps:

1. View the live version of your course.

2. Click on **Courseware** and navigate to the unit with the problem you want to review.

3. Display the problem and then click on the gray **SUBMISSION HISTORY** button below the problem (it will change to red when you hover over it).

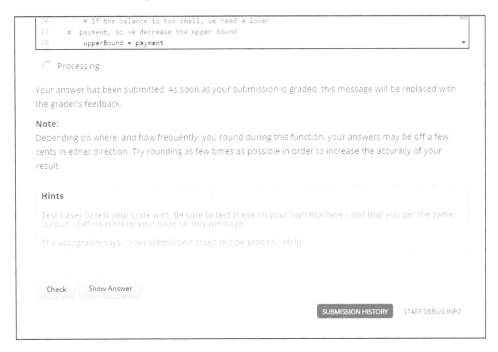

4. Enter the username of the student whose work you want to review, and then click on **View History** at the end of the page.

5. Close the **Submission History Viewer** by clicking outside it.

For certain problems, you can download a CSV file with data about the distribution of student answers. Student answer distribution data is available for these problem types:

- Checkboxes (`<choiceresponse>`)
- Dropdowns (`<optionresponse>`)
- Multiple choice (`<multiplechoiceresponse>`)
- Numerical input (`<numericalresponse>`)
- Text input (`<stringresponse>`)
- Mathematical expression input (`<formularesponse>`)

The file includes a row for each problem-answer combination from students. So, if a problem has five possible answers, the file includes up to five rows—one for each answer selected by at least one student.

For problems with **Randomization** enabled (sometimes called re-randomization), there is one row for each problem-variant-and-answer combination.

An automated process periodically runs on edX to update the CSV file containing the student answer data. A link to the most recently updated version is available on the **Instructor Dashboard**. You can access the link as follows:

1. View the live version of your course.

2. Click on **Instructor** and then on **Data Download**.

3. Click on the `{course_id}_answer_distribution.csv` file at the bottom of the page.

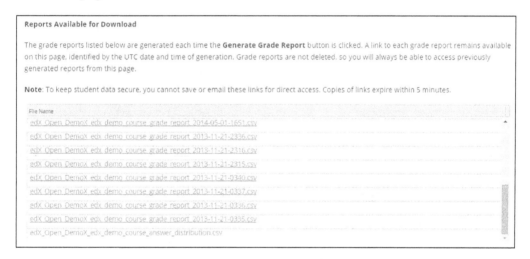

You can also view a chart of the score distribution for a specified problem but, to view the score distribution for a problem, you will need its unique identifier. You can display a histogram for problems that have the `/problem/` prefix in the unique identifier.

To display the distribution of scores for a problem, perform these steps:

1. View the live version of your course.

2. Click on **Instructor** and then on **Analytics**.

3. Select a problem by using its unique identifier in the **SCORE DISTRIBUTION** section.

 The **Analytics** page updates to display a histogram of scores for that problem.

Gradebook management

You can review how grading is configured for your course and access student grades whenever you want. You can also adjust student grading for a problem, a student, or all students.

You can review the assignment types that are graded and their respective weights using the **Instructor Dashboard**. While your edX course is in progress, you can view an XML representation of the assignment types in your course and how they are weighted to determine students' grades. To do so, follow these steps:

1. View the live version of your course.

2. Click on **Instructor** and then on **Data Download**.

3. Select the gray **Grading Configuration** button.

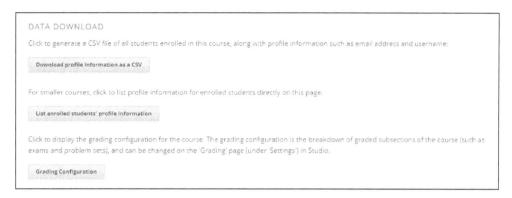

4. A list of the assignment types in your course shows up.

 In this example, Homework is weighted as 0.3 (30 percent) of the grade. In Studio, you can define this information by selecting **Settings** and then **Grading**.

```
Click to display the grading configuration for the course. The grading configuration is the breakdown of graded subsections of the course (such as
exams and problem sets), and can be changed on the 'Grading' page (under 'Settings') in Studio.

  Grading Configuration

-----------------------------------------------------------------------
Course grader:
<class 'xmodule.graders.WeightedSubsectionsGrader'>

Graded sections:
   subgrader=<class 'xmodule.graders.AssignmentFormatGrader'>, type=Homework, category=Homework, weight=0.75
   subgrader=<class 'xmodule.graders.AssignmentFormatGrader'>, type=, category=, weight=0.0
-----------------------------------------------------------------------
Listing grading context for course edX/Open_DemoX/edx_demo_course
graded sections:
[u'Exam', u'Homework']
--> Section Exam:
    Demo Course Overview (format=Exam, Assignment=)
    edX Exams (format=Exam, Assignment=)
--> Section Homework:
    Homework - Question Styles (format=Homework, Assignment=Ex 01)
    Homework - Labs and Demos (format=Homework, Assignment=Ex 02)
all descriptors:
length=83
```

For any course, you can generate grades and then download a file with the results for each enrolled student; here's how:

1. Click on **Instructor** and then on **Data Download**.

2. Select **Generate Grade Report** to start the grading process.

 A status message indicates that the grading process is in progress. This can take some time to complete, but you can navigate away from this page and do other work while it runs.

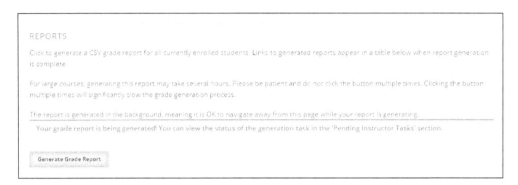

REPORTS

Click to generate a CSV grade report for all currently enrolled students. Links to generated reports appear in a table below when report generation is complete.

For large courses, generating this report may take several hours. Please be patient and do not click the button multiple times. Clicking the button multiple times will significantly slow the grade generation process.

The report is generated in the background, meaning it is OK to navigate away from this page while your report is generating.

Your grade report is being generated! You can view the status of the generation task in the 'Pending Instructor Tasks' section.

Generate Grade Report

3. Track the progress of the grading process by reloading the page in your browser and scrolling down to the **PENDING INSTRUCTION TASKS** section.

PENDING INSTRUCTOR TASKS

The status for any active tasks appears in a table below

Task Type	Task Inputs	Task ID	Requester	Submitted	Duration (sec)	State	Task Status	Task Progress
grade_course	{}	0ed5eda7-baab-44d6-8e2d-97b6ab7246d9	staff	2015-03-10T06:57:36+00:00	unknown	QUEUING	Incomplete	No status information available

4. Click on the link in the **File Name** area at the bottom of the page to the `{course_id}_grade_report_{date}.csv` file that displays the date you ran the grade report.

File Name

5. Open and review the CSV file.

The CSV file contains one row of data for each student, and columns that provide the following information:

- Student identifiers, including an internal ID, e-mail address, and username.

- The overall score attained in the course, expressed as a decimal value.

- Each {assignment type} {number} defined in your grading configuration, with the score a student earned for that specific assignment.

- An {assignment type} Avg with each student's current average score for that assignment type.

- A **Cohort Name** column — if cohorts are used — with the name of the cohort that each student belongs to, including the default. This column is empty for students who are not yet assigned to a cohort.

- An **Experiment Group** column — if content experiments are used — with the name of the experiment group that a student belongs to. The column heading includes the name of the group configuration. This column is empty for students who are not assigned to an experiment group. If your course has more than one experiment group, you will see one column for each group configuration.

For courses with up to 200 students, review the gradebook on the **Instructor Dashboard**:

1. View the live version of your course.

2. Click on **Instructor** and then on **Student Admin**.

 For courses with fewer than 200 students, this tab includes a **Student Gradebook** section.

3. Click on **View Gradebook**.

 Grades are calculated, and the gradebook is displayed.

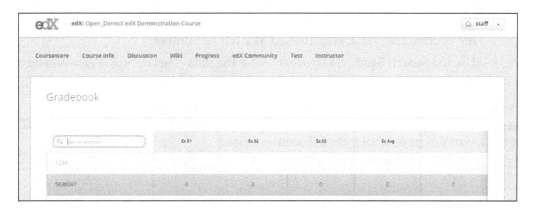

The gradebook includes the following features:

- Clicking on the username of a student displays their **Course Progress** page:

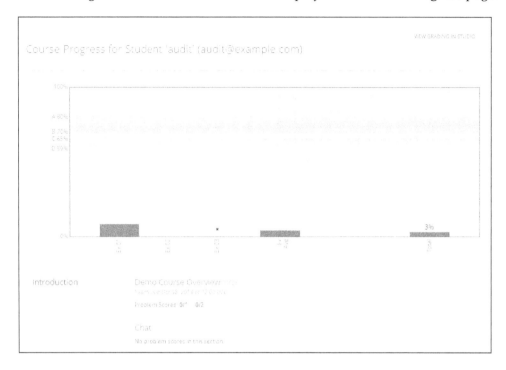

- There is a column for each {assignment type} {number} defined in your grading configuration, with the scores attained for that specific assignment.

- The gradebook does not have a scroll bar. To see the columns, click on the gradebook and drag it to left or right to reveal those columns.

- For assignment types that include more than one assignment, an {assignment type} Avg column displays each student's current average score.

- The **Total** column presents the total score a student has currently attained in the course. This value is expressed as a whole number.

- Use the **Search Students** option to filter the data. This option is case-sensitive and limits the rows displayed to usernames matching your entry.

Students can review their progress in your course by clicking on **Progress** in the navigation bar. Their progress through the graded part of the course gets displayed at the top of this page, above the subsection scores.

Progress is shown as a chart with entries for assignments, the total percentage earned, and the percentage needed for each grade cutoff. Students see the same visualization of their progress as you do.

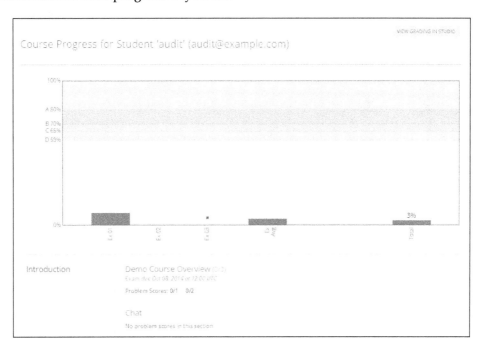

Student grades could be affected if you modify a problem or its settings after students have submitted an answer. If that happens, you can make the following adjustments to recalculate the grades of affected students when a correction or some other change is made:

- Rescore the submitted answer. You can rescore a problem for one student or all students enrolled in the course.

- Reset the number of times a student has attempted to answer the problem to zero so that the student can try again. You can reset the number of attempts for a single student or all students enrolled in the course.

- Delete a student's database history, or state, completely for the problem. You can delete student state for only one student at a time.

To make adjustments to student grades, you need the unique location identifier of the modified problem. When you create problems for your course, edX assigns them a unique location. To make grading adjustments for a problem, or to view data about it, you need to specify its location. Here's how to find the unique location identifier of a problem:

1. View the live version of your course.

2. Click on **Courseware** and navigate to the unit that contains the problem.

3. Display the problem and then click on **STAFF DEBUG INFO**.

 Information about the problem shows up, including its location.

4. To copy the location of the problem, select the entire location, right-click, and choose **Copy**. Close the **Staff Debug** viewer by clicking outside it.

If you need to rescore a problem for a single student, you need that student's username or e-mail address. Once you have that information, follow these steps:

1. View the live version of your course.

2. Click on **Courseware** and navigate to the component with the problem to rescore.

3. Display the problem and then click on **STAFF DEBUG INFO**. The **Staff Debug** viewer will open.

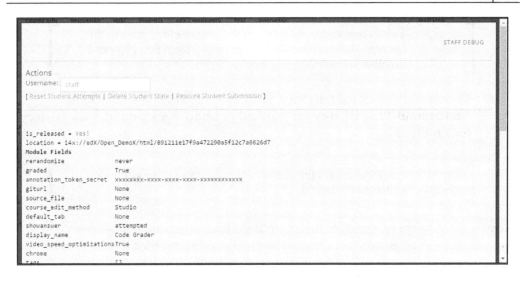

4. Enter the student's e-mail address or username in the **Username** field.

5. Click on **RESCORE STUDENT SUBMISSION**. Now, a message indicates successful adjustment.

6. Close the **Staff Debug** viewer by clicking outside it.

If you need to rescore submissions for all students, you first need the problem's location identifier. Once you have that in hand, here are the steps to be done:

1. View the live version of your course.

2. Click on **Instructor** and then on **Student Admin**.

3. Enter the unique problem location in the **COURSE-SPECIFIC GRADE ADJUSTMENT** section of the page, and then click on **Rescore ALL students' problem submissions**.

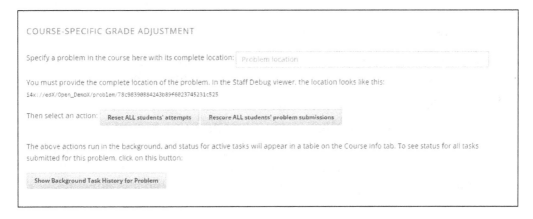

This process can take some time to complete. It runs in the background, so you can navigate away from this page and do other work while it runs.

4. View the results of the rescoring process by clicking on either **Show Background Task History for Student** or **Show Background Task History for Problem**.

 A table displays the status of the rescoring process for each student or problem.

To reset the number of attempts for a single student, you need that student's username or e-mail address. With that information you can then do the following:

1. View the live version of your course.

2. Click on **Courseware** and navigate to the component with the problem you want to reset.

3. Display the problem and then click on **STAFF DEBUG INFO**.

 The **Staff Debug** viewer will open.

4. Enter the student's e-mail address or username in the **Username** field.

5. Click on **Reset Student Attempts**.

 Now a message indicates successful adjustment.

6. To close the **Staff Debug** viewer, click outside it.

To reset the number of attempts that all enrolled students have for a problem, you need the unique identifier of the problem. You can then follow these steps:

1. View the live version of your course.

2. Click on **Instructor** and then on **Student Admin**.

3. Work in the **COURSE-SPECIFIC GRADE ADJUSTMENT** section of the page to reset the number of attempts for all enrolled students. Enter the unique problem location. Then click on **Reset ALL students' attempts**.

4. Click on **OK** when a dialog opens to indicate that the reset process is in progress.

 This process can take some time to complete. It runs in the background, so you can navigate away from this page and do other work while it runs.

5. View the results of the reset process by clicking on either **Show Background Task History for Student** or **Show Background Task History for Problem**.

To delete a student's entire history for a problem, you need that student's username or e-mail address. Student data is deleted permanently by this process; this action can't be undone. You can use either the **Staff Debug** viewer or **Instructor Dashboard** to delete a student's state.

To use the **Staff Debug** viewer, perform the following steps:

1. View the live version of your course.
2. Click on **Courseware** and navigate to the component containing the problem.
3. Display the problem and then click on **STAFF DEBUG INFO**.

 The **Staff Debug** viewer will open.

4. Enter the student's e-mail address or username in the **Username** field.
5. Click on **Delete Student State**.

 A message indicates successful adjustment.

6. Close the **Staff Debug** viewer by clicking outside it.

To use the **Instructor Dashboard**, you need the unique identifier of the problem. With that obtained you can then do the following:

1. Click on **Instructor** and then on **Student Admin**.
2. Enter both the student's -email address or username and the unique problem identifier in the **STUDENT-SPECIFIC GRADE ADJUSTMENT** section of the page.
3. Click on **Delete Student State for Problem**.

Completion certificates

To assign a final grade, generate the grades after the **Course End Date and Time** have passed. The final grades of a student in the course and the grading configuration you set in Studio determine whether the student has earned a certificate of mastery. The process of issuing certificates is thus complete at edX.

 Work with your edX program manager to schedule a date to issue certificates and complete this process.

Summary

With the emphasis on facilitating your course in this chapter, the last chapter focused on edX operations. You learned about the participants and related processes in your edX course. We also reviewed messaging your students and administering their grades; along the way we detailed managing course discussions and creating your course's Wiki. The chapter also dealt with course data and the criteria for course completion certificates.

Looking ahead, it's important to remember that, although you've invested a great deal of effort into your edX course, this alone won't guarantee that students will sign up. The solution is to promote your course using traditional and nontraditional marketing tactics. Therefore, as a value-added bonus, in *Chapter 8, Promoting Your Course* — the final chapter in this book — we will step outside our roles as educators and explore methods to market our edX course and personally brand ourselves. Covering traditional marketing tools, edX's marketing options, social media marketing strategies, personal branding, marketing metrics, and student feedback, *Chapter 8, Promoting Your Course,* will offer you actionable ideas and robust marketing resources.

8
Promoting Your Course

In the 1989 movie *Field of Dreams*, Ray Kinsella — the main character played by Kevin Costner — is told by a mysterious voice that "If you build it, he will come." The premise is that if he builds a baseball field in his corn field, then his late father, with whom he had a troubled relationship, will appear. After a mystical adventure, he builds the field, and not only does his father materialize, but other deceased baseball players arrive as well.

Unfortunately, as wonderful a movie as *Field of Dreams* is, you most likely won't have that same experience with your edX course. Just because you build it doesn't mean students will materialize out of thin air like the baseball players in that movie. The solution is to promote your course using traditional and nontraditional marketing tactics.

To help you with this final step, this chapter suggests strategies you can use to promote your edX course to increase enrollment and improve engagement among future, current, and former students alike. From social media to networking with students, this chapter offers actionable approaches and sensible strategies to attract students. To accomplish this, in this chapter you will learn how to:

- Tackle traditional marketing tools
- Explore edX's marketing options
- Survey social media marketing
- Better understand personal branding
- Maximize marketing metrics
- Leverage student feedback

Traditional marketing tools

Sometimes, it's easy to overlook the obvious. Such is the case with marketing your edX course. Given its technical nature, it's possible to disregard or overlook traditional promotional possibilities.

Granted, these will likely have a somewhat limited reach, but they do have value. You might notice that traditional tools are especially useful for a course offered only to students at your university or in a small private online course (SPOC). In a corporate setting, they might be all that is needed, especially since there is no need to market a class outside an organization.

Of course, you shouldn't interpret the use of the word *traditional* here to mean offline; rather think of it as meaning *established*. We will explore social media marketing options in the *Social media marketing* section of this chapter.

Given this, before (or at least in addition to) pursuing online promotional efforts and social media marketing options, consider the following traditional marketing tools:

- **Bulletin boards**: Post flyers on campus billboards, making sure that you have detachable pieces at the bottom with a short URL linking to the course.

- **Businesses partnerships**: Ask local businesses to post flyers for your course or explore incentives, contests, or other ways they can promote your course. Depending on the subject matter of your course, you might consider including the business as a case study or some other component of the curriculum.

- **Campus media**: Place a display ad in your university's newspaper with the entire course information. Also consider asking the editor to have a reporter interview you about your course. Record a promo for your campus's radio station or ask to be interviewed as a guest on one of the station's shows. Get a commercial produced by your campus or community TV station, or arrange to be interviewed much like the campus radio station.

 Read about advertising an event on campus in the article *Where to Advertise an Event on Campus* at `http://collegelife. about.com/od/cocurricularlife/a/Where-To- Advertise-An-Event-On-Campus.htm`.

- **Direct mail**: Announce your course to students, colleagues, and friends with a postcard or letter, making sure that you include all of the course information.

You can increase your knowledge of direct mail and related concepts by visiting the website of *Direct Marketing News*, a magazine focused on the direct marketing industry, at `http://www.dmnews.com`.

- **E-mail newsletters**: This is similar to direct mail, but is sent by e-mail. Just be careful to remain compliant with the rules and requirements of the CAN-SPAM Act.

You can learn more about the CAN-SPAM Act at `http://www.ftc.gov/tips-advice/business-center/guidance/can-spam-act-compliance-guide-business`.

- **Intranets or private networks**: An Intranet or private network offers private companies that use edX for internal training across several offices and schools alike an efficient option for sharing information with many individuals.

You can learn more about Intranets by reading the article *How Intranets Work* at `http://computer.howstuffworks.com/how-intranets-work3.htm`. You might also find some insight in the scholarly paper *Intranets: Catalysts for Improved Organizational Communication*, which you can download from `http://bit.ly/IntranetsCatalysts`.

- **Movie theater advertisements**: Most movie theaters now run advertisements — typically a display ad — before they start the feature film. This could be an affordable and effective option for you.

Learn more about advertising options in movie theaters by reading the latest research from the Cinema Advertising Council at `http://www.cinemaadcouncil.org/cac_researchMain.php`. Also explore the websites of the two largest providers of on-screen advertising: NCM Media Network at `http://www.ncm.com` and Screenvision at `http://www.screenvision.com`.

- **Windshield flyers**: This is likely a relatively ineffective and annoying option (not to mention environmentally unfriendly) but, if you strategically select parking lots where potential students are most likely to be, you might have some success.

- **Word of mouth**: Cost-effective for marketers and trusted by consumers, word-of-mouth is one of your best bets. In this situation, former students can become your marketing mouthpieces. Be sure to request them to tell their friends if they have had a positive experience in your class. Word of mouth is intertwined with student feedback; refer to the *Student feedback* section later in this chapter to learn how to leverage it to your advantage.

 Improve your understanding of word of mouth marketing by reviewing the resources on the website-of-the Word of Mouth Marketing Association at `http://www.womma.org/resources`.

Marketing resources

For additional marketing insight and information, consider consulting the following articles and resources:

- *7 Golden Steps to Creating an Effective Email Newsletter*:
  `http://www.verticalresponse.com/blog/7-golden-steps-to-creating-an-effective-email-newsletter/`

- The American Marketing Association's resources page:
  `https://www.ama.org/resources/Pages/default.aspx`

- Andrew Careaga's Higher Ed Marketing blog:
  `https://andrewcareaga.wordpress.com/`

- *Bob Johnson's Blog on Higher Education Marketing:*
  `http://www.bobjohnsonblog.com/`

- *Creating A Thoughtful Content Strategy in Higher Education Marketing*:
  `http://blog.hubspot.com/marketing/creating-thoughtful-content-strategy-higher-education-marketing`

- *Higher Ed Marketing Journal*:
  `http://higheredmarketingjournal.com/`

- Higher Education Marketing Blog:
  `http://www.higher-education-marketing.com/`

- *How to Avoid Turning Off Traditional Stakeholders in Higher Education Marketing*:
  `http://blog.hubspot.com/marketing/avoid-turning-off-traditional-stakeholders-higher-education-marketing`

- *Principles of Marketing Tutorials*:
  `http://www.knowthis.com/principles-of-marketing-tutorials`

- *How to Create an Email Newsletter People Actually Read*:
  `http://blog.hubspot.com/marketing/guide-creating-email-newsletters-ht`

- Marketing articles by Marketing Profs:
  `http://www.marketingprofs.com/marketing/library/articles/`

edX's marketing options

In the *Messages to students* section of *Chapter 7, Facilitating Your Course*, we discussed the use of weekly messages about the course to inform your students. While that's an effective way to keep your current students engaged in class, if you don't market your course, you might not get any new students to teach. Fortunately, edX provides you with an array of tools for this purpose, as follows:

- **Creative Submission Tool**: Submit the assets required for creating a page in your edX course using the Creative Submission Tool. You can also use those very materials in promoting the course.

 Access the Creative Submission Tool at `https://edx.projectrequest.net/index.php/request`.

- **Logo and the Media Kit**: Although these are intended for members of the media, you can also use the edX Media Kit for your promotional purposes: you can download high-resolution photos, edX logo visual guidelines (in Adobe Illustrator and EPS versions), key facts about edX, and answers to frequently asked questions. You can also contact the press office for additional information.

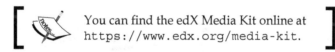 You can find the edX Media Kit online at `https://www.edx.org/media-kit`.

- **edX Learner Stories**: Using stories of students who have succeeded with other edX courses is a compelling way to market the potential of your course. Using Tumblr, edX Learner Stories offers more than a dozen student profiles. You might want to use their stories directly or use them as a template for marketing materials of your own.

 Read edX Learner Stories at `http://edxstories.tumblr.com`.

Social media marketing

Traditional marketing tools and the options available in the edX Marketing Portal are a fitting first step in promoting your course. However, social media gives you a tremendously enhanced toolkit you can use to attract, convert, and transform spectators into students.

When marketing your course with social media, you will also simultaneously create a digital footprint for yourself. This in turn helps establish your subject matter expertise far beyond one edX course. What's more, you won't be alone; there exists a large community of edX instructors and students, including those from other MOOC platforms already online.

Take, for example, the following screenshot from edX's Twitter account (@edxonline). edX has embraced social media as a means of marketing and to create a practising virtual community for those creating and taking their courses.

Likewise, edX also actively maintains a page on Facebook, as follows:

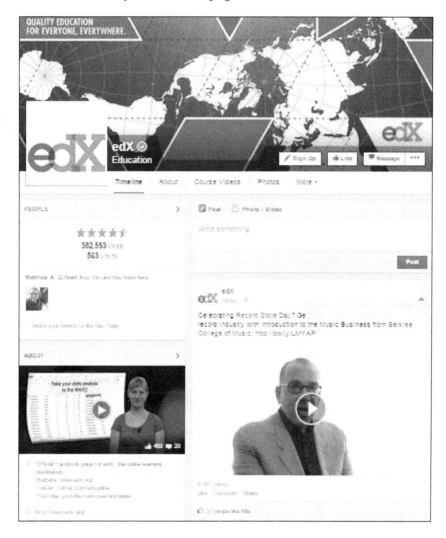

You can also see how active edX's YouTube channel is in the following screenshot. Note that there are both educational and promotional videos.

To get you started in social media—if you're not already there—take a look at the list of 12 social media tools, as follows. Not all of these tools might be relevant to your needs, but consider the suggestions to decide how you might best use them, and give them a try:

- **Facebook** (https://www.facebook.com): Create a fan page for your edX course; you can re-use content from your course's About page such as your course intro video, course description, course image, and any other relevant materials. Be sure to include a link from the Facebook page for your course to its About page. Look for ways to share other content from your course (or related to your course) in a way that engages members of your fan page. Use your Facebook page to generate interest and answer questions from potential students. You might also consider creating a Facebook group. This can be more useful for current students to share knowledge during the class and to network once it's complete.

Visit edX on Facebook at `https://www.facebook.com/edX`.

- **Google+** (`https://plus.google.com`): Take the same approach as you did with your Facebook fan page. While this is not as engaging as Facebook, you might find that posting content on Google+ increases traffic to your course's About page due to the increased referrals you are likely to experience via Google search results.

 Add edX to your circles on Google+ at `https://plus.google.com/+edXOnline/posts`.

- **Instagram** (`https://instagram.com`): Share behind-the-scenes pictures of you and your staff for your course. Show your students what a day in your life is like, making sure to use a unique hashtag for your course.

 Picture the possibilities with edX on Instagram at `https://instagram.com/edxonline/`.

- **LinkedIn** (`https://www.linkedin.com`): Share information about your course in relevant LinkedIn groups, and post public updates about it in your personal account. Again, make sure you include a unique hashtag for your course and a link to the About page.

 Connect with edX on LinkedIn at `https://www.linkedin.com/company/edx`.

- **Pinterest** (`https://www.pinterest.com`): Share photos as with Instagram, but also consider sharing infographics about your course's subject matter or share infographics or imagers you use in your actual course as well. You might consider creating pin boards for each course, or one per pin board per module in a course.

 Pin edX onto your Pinterest pin board at `https://www.pinterest.com/edxonline/`.

- **Slideshare** (http://www.slideshare.net): If you want to share your subject matter expertise and thought leadership with a wider audience, Slideshare is a great platform to use. You can easily post your PowerPoint presentations, class documents or scholarly papers, infographics, and videos from your course or another topic. All of these can then be shared across other social media platforms.

 Review presentations from or about edX courses on Slideshare at http://www.slideshare.net/search/slideshow?searchfrom=header&q=edx.

- **SoundCloud** (https://soundcloud.com): With SoundCloud, you can share MP3 files of your course lectures or create podcasts related to your areas of expertise. Your work can be shared on Twitter, Tumblr, Facebook, and Foursquare, expanding your influence and audience exponentially.

 Listen to some audio content from Harvard University at https://soundcloud.com/harvard.

- **Tumblr** (https://www.tumblr.com): Resembling what the child of WordPress and Twitter might be like, Tumblr provides a platform to share behind-the-scenes text, photos, quotes, links, chat, audios, and videos of your edX course and the people who make it possible. Share a "day in the life" or document in real time, an interactive history of each edX course you teach.

 Read edX's learner stories at http://edxstories.tumblr.com.

- **Twitter** (https://twitter.com): Although messages on Twitter are limited to 140 characters, one tweet can have a big impact. For a faculty wanting to promote its edX course, it is an efficient and cost-effective option. Tweet course videos, samples of content, links to other curriculum, or promotional material. Engage with other educators who teach courses and retweet posts from academic institutions.

 Follow edX on Twitter at https://twitter.com/edxonline. You might also consider subscribing to edX's Twitter list of edX instructors at https://twitter.com/edXOnline/lists/edx-professors, and explore the Twitter accounts of edX courses by subscribing to that list at https://twitter.com/edXOnline/lists/edx-courses.

- **Vine** (`https://vine.co`): A short-format video service owned by Twitter, Vine provides you with 6 seconds to share your creativity, either in a continuous stream or smaller segments linked together like stop motion. You might create a vine showing the inner working of the course faculty and staff, or maybe even ask short questions related to the course content and invite people to reply with answers.

 Watch vines about MOOCs at `https://vine.co/tags/MOOC`.

- **WordPress**: WordPress gives you two options to manage and share content with students. With WordPress.com (`https://wordpress.com`), you're given a selection of standardized templates to use on a hosted platform. You have limited control but reasonable flexibility and limited, if any, expenses. With Wordpress.org (`https://wordpress.org`), you have more control but you need to host it on your own web server, which requires some technical know-how. The choice is yours.

 Read posts on edX on the MIT Open Matters blog on `Wordpress.com` at `https://mitopencourseware.wordpress.com/category/edx/`.

- **YouTube** (`https://www.youtube.com`): YouTube is the heart of your edX course. It's the core of your curriculum and the anchor of engagement for your students. When promoting your course, use existing videos from your curriculum in your social media campaigns, but identify opportunities to record short videos specifically for promoting your course.

 Watch course videos and promotional content on the edX YouTube channel at `https://www.youtube.com/user/EdXOnline`.

Social media marketing resources

If you want to learn more about social media marketing, check out these resources:

- *6 Tips for an Effective Pinterest Strategy:*
  `http://www.socialmediatoday.com/content/6-tips-effective-pinterest-strategy`

- *15 LinkedIn Marketing Hacks to Grow Your Business*:
  `http://www.businessnewsdaily.com/7206-linkedin-marketing-business.html`

- *26 Ways to Engage Your Fans on Facebook*: http://www.socialmediaexaminer.com/tag/facebook-content-strategy/

- *Facebook Success: 7 Strategies for Nonprofits*: http://www.slideshare.net/HubSpot/facebook-success-7-cheat-codes-for-nonprofits-22941998

- Hootsuite University's social media strategy videos: https://www.youtube.com/user/HootSuiteUniversity

- *How To Build A Winning Twitter Strategy In 2014*: http://www.forbes.com/sites/jaysondemers/2014/04/01/how-to-build-a-winning-twitter-strategy-in-2014/

- *How to Rock Instagram: Lessons from Adidas, Ben & Jerry's, and Other Top Brands*: http://contently.com/strategist/2014/05/29/how-to-rock-instagram-lessons-from-adidas-ben-jerrys-and-other-top-brands/

- *Ramon de Leon, Social Media Marketer at Dominos Pizza Energizes the Stage at LeWeb Paris 2012*: https://youtu.be/Tvf3LSER4Jw

- *The Marketer's Guide to Instagram*: http://www.entrepreneur.com/article/226014

- *The Twitter Small Business Blog*: https://blog.twitter.com/small-business

Personal branding basics

Additionally, whether the impact of your effort is immediately evident or not, your social media presence powers your personal brand as a professor. Why is that important? Read on to know.

With the possible exception of marketing professors, most educators likely tend to think more about creating and teaching their course than promoting it—or themselves. Traditionally, that made sense, but it isn't practical in today's digitally connected world. Social media opens an area of influence where all educators—especially those teaching an edX course—should be participating.

Unfortunately, many professors don't know where or how to start with social media. If you're teaching a course on edX, or even edX Edge, you will likely have some kind of marketing support from your university or edX. But if you are just in an organization using edX Code, or simply want to promote yourself and your edX course, you might be on your own.

One option to get you started with social media is the Babb Group, a provider of resources and consulting for online professors, business owners, and real-estate investors. Its founder and CEO, Dani Babb (PhD), says this:

"Social media helps you show that you are an expert in a given field. It is an important tool today to help you get hired, earn promotions, and increase your visibility."

The Babb Group offers five packages focused on different social media platforms: Twitter, LinkedIn, Facebook, Twitter and Facebook, or Twitter with Facebook and LinkedIn.

 You can view the Babb Group's social media marketing packages at http://www.thebabbgroup.com/social-media-profiles-for-professors.html. Connect with Dani Babb on LinkedIn at https://www.linkedin.com/in/drdanibabb or on Twitter at https://twitter.com/danibabb

Personal branding resources

To further explore the concept of personal branding and learn how you can better market yourself and your edX course, take a look at the following links:

- Five actionable personal branding tips for social media: https://blog.bufferapp.com/social-media-strategy-personal-branding-tips

- *5 Steps to Building a Personal Brand (and Why You Need One)*: http://www.inc.com/jayson-demers/5-steps-to-building-a-personal-brand-and-why-you-need-one.html

- *7 Things You Can Do To Build An Awesome Personal Brand*:
  http://www.forbes.com/sites/shamahyder/2014/08/18/7-things-you-can-do-to-build-an-awesome-personal-brand/

- *Building your personal brand*:
  http://www.pwc.com/us/en/careers/campus/programs-events/personal-brand/index.jhtml#overview

- Entrepreneur's articles on personal branding:
  http://www.entrepreneur.com/topic/personal-branding

- *How to Build an Unforgettable Personal Brand*, OPEN Forum:
  https://www.americanexpress.com/us/small-business/openforum/articles/how-to-build-an-unforgettable-personal-brand/

- *How to Build Your Personal Brand*:
  http://www.wikihow.com/Build-Your-Personal-Brand

- Personal Branding Blog:
  http://www.personalbrandingblog.com

- *The Complete Guide to Building Your Personal Brand*:
  http://www.quicksprout.com/the-complete-guide-to-building-your-personal-brand/

- *The lazy person's guide to personal branding*:
  http://mashable.com/2014/11/10/personal-branding-lazy-guide/

Marketing metrics

Without defining goals to measure your efforts against, it's hard to know how well you've succeeded, or even whether you've succeeded at all. That's why metrics for your marketing strategy are so important. Without benchmarks, you won't have empirical evidence to evaluate. You might be able to make anecdotal assumptions, but you will have nothing you can use to make definitive decisions.

Moreover, metrics alone can't always tell a complete story. For example, in baseball, hitting three out of ten balls pitched to you — 30 percent — is considered a good batting average. However, in an academic setting, the same percentage is well below a failing mark.

What's the difference? It's context. Without context, you don't understand the relativity of numbers and different datasets to each other. Therefore, when it comes to evaluating the metrics of your marketing, you always need to consider the context.

There is no single "right" answer where metrics are involved. The right answers are those that matter the most to you personally, or are most relevant to the goals you're trying to achieve.

In that spirit, you might find the following articles informative, but ultimately, you will need to define and measure your own metrics:

- *10 Online Marketing Metrics You Need To Be Measuring*: http://www.forbes.com/sites/jaysondemers/2014/08/15/10-online-marketing-metrics-you-need-to-be-measuring/

- *18 Marketing Performance Metrics that Matter*: http://www.themarketingscore.com/blog/bid/220074/18-Marketing-Performance-Metrics-that-Matter

- *7 Content Marketing Metrics You're Probably Undervaluing*: http://contently.com/strategist/2014/08/21/7-content-marketing-metrics-youre-probably-undervaluing/

- *Marketing Metrics Made Simple*: http://www.marketing-metrics-made-simple.com/

- Social media analytics at Mashable: http://mashable.com/category/social-media-analytics/

- *Social Media Metrics and ROI*: http://moz.com/beginners-guide-to-social-media/metrics-and-roi

- The Google Analytics blog: http://analytics.blogspot.com

- *The Social Media Metrics That Should Matter To Small Businesses*: http://blog.hootsuite.com/social-media-metrics-for-small-businesses/

- *Which Stats Matter: A Definitive Guide to Social Media Metrics*: https://blog.bufferapp.com/definitive-guide-social-media-metrics-stats

Student feedback

Feedback from students is an often overlooked source of actionable ideas. Instructors tend to overlook or underappreciate feedback from their students, but if you attempt to engage the essence of the ideas behind the feedback you receive, you might very well discover some implementable ideas.

Instructors are typically limited to the official feedback collected by the universities for which they're teaching. However, you don't have to limit yourself to that. Why not create your own end or course survey, or launch a survey midway through the course to gauge what is working and what is not?

How you collect feedback will vary based on your course, goals, and students. Just remember to collect both quantitative and qualitative feedback.

Some suggestions for collecting feedback are as follow:

- **Discussions**: The path of least resistance might just be to ask your students for feedback in a special discussion forum. It's not anonymous, so students might be less forthcoming. Also, if the feedback is in the form of comments in a discussion thread, it may be tough to collect, code, and analyze the data, but it might give you some anecdotal insight.

- **Modified edX problem component**: Create a problem component in a unit specifically created to collect any feedback from students. You can circumvent the grading process if you make every answer a correct one and just review the submissions directly.

- **Third-party surveys**: If you want to collect data accurately and usefully, your best bet is a third-party survey you can link to from your course.

Licensed and open source survey options include the following:

Licensed survey software	Links
Constant Contact	`http://search.constantcontact.com/online-surveys`
FluidSurveys	`http://fluidsurveys.com`
Polldaddy	`https://polldaddy.com/`
Poll Everywhere	`http://www.polleverywhere.com`
Qualtrics	`http://www.qualtrics.com`
Questionform	`http://questionform.com`
QuestionPro	`http://www.questionpro.com`
Snap Surveys	`http://www.snapsurveys.com`
SurveyGizmo	`http://www.surveygizmo.com`
SurveyMonkey	`http://www.surveymonkey.com`

Open source survey software	Links
Generic HTML Form Processor	`http://www.goeritz.net/brmic/`
Google Forms	`https://support.google.com/docs/answer/87809`
LimeSurvey	`http://www.limesurvey.org`
Opina	`https://opinahq.com`
Survey Project	`http://www.surveyproject.org`

Ultimately, the strongest measure of the value of student feedback is the degree to which you adapt in response to it. Carefully consider the outliers—comments that are either too negative or overly gratuitous. They might give you some insight, but are often not constructive (for example, "I learned nothing at all in this class"); or they lavish tremendous praise without any actionable insight (for example, "This was the best class ever; my life will never be the same!). Instead, focus more of your energy identifying patterns such as students saying essentially the same thing in different ways, or the same comment appearing multiple times (either positive or negative). Be open minded to the input, realizing — as any good marketer would — that your students are your customers and you should be mindful of their needs and wants, while not sacrificing academic integrity or rigor.

[To learn more about designing a survey, read the article *How to Create a Survey* at http://www.wikihow.com/Create-a-Survey.]

Summary

In this chapter, we discussed strategies to help you market your edX course before it is offered, and to create networking opportunities for your students after it concludes. From social media to networking with students, this chapter offered actionable approaches and sensible strategies to attract students.

We tackled traditional marketing tools, identified options available from edX, discussed social media marketing, explored personal branding basics, reviewed making and measuring marketing metrics, and defined the role of student feedback in marketing your courses.

This book was designed to walk you through the steps to create your first course with edX. With the core content of this book complete, the next steps are yours to take. You should have a strong sense of your strategy and an understanding of your options. You should feel confident about developing or adapting your curriculum, producing instructional videos, designing exercises and assessments, and administering your course while marketing it with social media.

Remember that this will be a learning process as well. You can't expect to understand every nuance of the system, nor can you anticipate all the issues you might encounter. Also realize that, as a cloud-based system, edX will always be in the midst of updates and evolution. Embrace it and work with it; after all, you are a lifelong learner, right?

Enjoy teaching your edX course. May it be an edXcellent adventure!

Index

Symbols

3Play Media
  URL 91
.tar.gz files
  URL 202

A

About page
  about 46, 47
  About video 57
  across edX versions 47
  descriptive picture 54
  Frequently Asked Questions (FAQ) 53, 54
  long course description 48
  other course information 60, 61
  prerequisites 52, 53
  short course description 49
  short course description, staff
       biographies 50-52
About video
  about 57
  adding 58-60
A/B split testing
  URL 120
accessibility issues
  about 178
  reference links 178
advanced components
  adding, to edX course 140-144
answer data
  about 245
  problem distribution scores,
       displaying 247, 248

reviewing 245-247
assessments 66-68

B

back light 82
best practices, YouTube 92-94
Beta Tester
  about 198
  individual Beta Tester, adding 198
  multiple Beta Testers, adding 199, 200
  removing 200, 201
beta testing
  about 197
  course, accessing 197
  feedback, evaluating 197
  finishing 197
  planning 197
  recruiting 197
  roles, assigning 197

C

CAN-SPAM Act
  URL 261
completion certificates
  issuing 258
components, edX course
  advanced components, adding 140
  discussion components,
       adding 139-147
  HTML components, adding 139-151
  problem components, adding 140, 151
  video components, adding 140, 152-155

X

XBlock Google group
  URL, for forum 11, 205

Y

YouTube
  best practices 92-94
  caption editor, URL 92
  edX course, URL 269
  URL 269

Thank you for buying
edX E-Learning Course Development

About Packt Publishing

Packt, pronounced 'packed', published its first book, *Mastering phpMyAdmin for Effective MySQL Management*, in April 2004, and subsequently continued to specialize in publishing highly focused books on specific technologies and solutions.

Our books and publications share the experiences of your fellow IT professionals in adapting and customizing today's systems, applications, and frameworks. Our solution-based books give you the knowledge and power to customize the software and technologies you're using to get the job done. Packt books are more specific and less general than the IT books you have seen in the past. Our unique business model allows us to bring you more focused information, giving you more of what you need to know, and less of what you don't.

Packt is a modern yet unique publishing company that focuses on producing quality, cutting-edge books for communities of developers, administrators, and newbies alike. For more information, please visit our website at www.packtpub.com.

About Packt Open Source

In 2010, Packt launched two new brands, Packt Open Source and Packt Enterprise, in order to continue its focus on specialization. This book is part of the Packt Open Source brand, home to books published on software built around open source licenses, and offering information to anybody from advanced developers to budding web designers. The Open Source brand also runs Packt's Open Source Royalty Scheme, by which Packt gives a royalty to each open source project about whose software a book is sold.

Writing for Packt

We welcome all inquiries from people who are interested in authoring. Book proposals should be sent to author@packtpub.com. If your book idea is still at an early stage and you would like to discuss it first before writing a formal book proposal, then please contact us; one of our commissioning editors will get in touch with you.

We're not just looking for published authors; if you have strong technical skills but no writing experience, our experienced editors can help you develop a writing career, or simply get some additional reward for your expertise.

Odoo Development Essentials

ISBN: 978-1-78439-279-6   Paperback: 214 pages

Fast track your development skills to build powerful Odoo business applications

1. Leverage the powerful and rapid development Odoo framework to build the perfect app for your business needs.

2. Learn to use models, views, and business logic to assemble solid business applications effectively.

3. Get up and running with Odoo and integrate it with external data and applications using this easy-to-follow guide.

Ext JS Essentials

ISBN: 978-1-78439-662-6   Paperback: 216 pages

Get up and running with building interactive and rich web applications using Sencha's Ext JS 5

1. Learn the Ext JS framework for developing rich web applications.

2. Understand how the framework works under the hood.

3. Explore the main tools and widgets of the framework for use in your own applications.

Please check **www.PacktPub.com** for information on our titles

www.ingramcontent.com/pod-product-compliance
Lightning Source LLC
Chambersburg PA
CBHW062109050326
40690CB00016B/3264